On the edge:
Britain and Europe

Hugh Dykes Brendan Donnelly

First published in 2012 by Forumpress

Forumpress
c/o The Global Policy Institute
London Metropolitan University
31 Jewry Street
London EC3N 2EY, UK

ISBN: 978-1-907144-07-3

A catalogue record for this book is available from the British Library

For further information on Forumpress visit our website:
www.forumpress.co.uk

Design and Layout: Fred Fieber www.fredfieber.co.uk

Printing by Remous Limited www.remous.com

The Authors

Hugh Dykes was the Conservative MP for Harrow from 1970 to 1997. He served as Chairman of the Conservative Group for Europe and of the Commons Tory MP's Committee. He is now spokesman for the Liberal Democrats in the House of Lords, becoming a peer in 2004.

Brendan Donnelly was a Conservative Member of the European Parliament from 1994 to 1999. He left the Conservative Party in 1999 in protest against the Party's growing Euroscepticism. He has since written and spoken widely on European affairs. He stood in the European Elections of 2009 as a candidate for the party Yes2Europe.

Contents

Introduction

In the early morning of 9th December 2011, the patience of Britain's European partners finally ran out. In return for his acquiescence in the drawing up of a new European treaty to save the Eurozone, Mr. Cameron demanded a number of special arrangements for the United Kingdom to 'protect the City of London' against the consequences of future European financial regulation. Mr. Cameron (mis)calculated that other countries were so eager to have a treaty at the level of twenty-seven that they would be prepared to pay a stiff price to Britain for this to happen, allowing Britain to veto in the future directives and other regulation in the financial sector which are currently decided by qualified majority vote.

Britain's partners however were in no mood to be blackmailed. Britain had been vocal in calling for changes to improve the functioning of the Eurozone; these treaty changes would have no impact on Britain as a non-member of the Eurozone; in many European countries the City of London is regarded as a source of continent-wide economic instability, which needs to be reined in; and the presentation of the British demands to the European Council was clumsy and provocative. All these factors led to the brusque rejection of the British demands and the decision that all Britain's twenty-six partners would agree between themselves a separate treaty enshrining the measures they thought appropriate to protect the Eurozone. Many observers understandably regard this episode as an important step towards Britain's eventual (and perhaps not so eventual) departure from the European Union altogether.

Mr. Cameron's 'veto' was enthusiastically welcomed by his most misoEuropean colleagues in the House of Commons. They overlooked or had not realised that the City of London is now in formal terms no more or less 'at risk' than it was before the European Council. Mr. Cameron's attempts to obtain special arrangements for the City failed entirely. In informal terms, goodwill from our partners towards the City and the British government has certainly not been enhanced by these events, but rather diminished. This lessened goodwill will probably be reflected, to the disadvantage of the City, in all European discussion of financial regulation over the coming months. Far from protecting the interests of the City of London, Mr. Cameron has in fact placed them at some risk by his irresponsible attempt to placate his friends in the City and his political opponents in his own party. He would do well to remember the Churchillian dictum that feeding the crocodile at best ensures that he will eat you last.

Mr. Cameron's blundering alienation of all his European partners is the tragic culmination of two decades of political controversy in this country concerning the European Union. During those decades the British discussion of European issues has increasingly lost any contact with reality or rationality. A toxic cocktail of wilful ignorance, political opportunism and media manipulation has distorted the European debate to such an extent that even those in theory favourable to a central and constructive British role in the European Union have found themselves endorsing many of the premises of their opponents. In this short book, a number of the elements in this poisonous cocktail will be critically reviewed. It will become depressingly clear through this review that Britain's position within the Union is currently in great jeopardy; and that those who sincerely wish to maintain and consolidate this position need fundamentally to reconsider the tactics and rhetoric they have employed until now.

Chapter One:
An unlikely coalition

As the General Election campaign of 2010 neared its end, it began to seem increasingly plausible that no single party would have an overall majority in the House of Commons. Favoured hypotheses included a minority government of the largest party in the House of Commons, presumably the Conservatives; a Coalition between the probable second and third largest parties, the Labour Party and the Liberal Democrats; and a pact between the Conservatives and the Liberal Democrats, whereby the latter would facilitate the formation of a minority Conservative government to deal with the United Kingdom's urgent economic problems, but would not themselves participate in government. It came as a surprise to many commentators, and indeed to many voters, that the consequence of the General Election held on 6th

May 2010 was a full-scale Coalition between the Conservative Party and the Liberal Democrats.

There had been good reason for this failure of prediction. Much of the electoral success of the Liberal Democrats in recent years stemmed from their ability to win over traditional Labour voters disappointed by New Labour's lack of radicalism. Few Liberal Democrats, whether MPs or party members, would quarrel with the description of their party as being from the 'left of centre'. This might have been expected to predispose them to seek an alliance with the Labour Party in a 'hung' Parliament. On the most salient issue of the campaign, the pace, scale and manner of the painful decisions necessary to reduce the public debt, the Liberal Democrats seemed nearer the Labour Party than the more radical Conservative Party.

Nor was public expenditure the only issue which seemed likely to block any participation of Liberal Democrat ministers in a predominantly Conservative cabinet. Since it left office in 1997, the Conservative Party had become increasingly hostile to European integration. The Liberal Democrats were by common accord the most pro-European of the British parties. European policy seemed one of the most menacing rocks upon which any proposal for a Coalition government of the Liberal Democrats and the Conservatives was likely to founder.

The negotiations after the general election between the Liberal Democrats and the Conservatives rapidly proved that the supposedly unbridgeable policy differences between the two parties had been much exaggerated. Agreement on a wide range of issues was efficiently achieved by the negotiators of the two parties and on 11th

May David Cameron became the twelfth Prime Minister of Queen Elizabeth II. Criticism of the Liberals for their participation in the Coalition centred on the proposed economic policy of the new government, a policy which Nick Clegg and his colleagues depicted before the General Election as likely severely to damage the British economy.

Scarcely a murmur was raised against an equally dramatic retreat in the Coalition agreement from what had previously been held as central Liberal Democratic principles, those relating to European policy. That was powerful evidence of the changes wrought in British public and political opinion by twenty years of political feeble-mindedness on the European issue by politicians and opinion-formers. Nobody who reads the Coalition agreement with an open mind can see it as other than a recipe for the consolidation and even reinforcement of the United Kingdom's semi-detached position within the European Union. But all too many of those proclaiming themselves (relatively) ardent enthusiasts for British participation in the European Union accepted at the time the agreement's self-marginalising provisions with resignation, or even with relief that these provisions were not yet more damaging. In line after line of its text, the agreement perfectly mirrored all that is most confused, incoherent and damaging in British attitudes towards the European Union.

–o0o–

The rebarbative introductory paragraph of the agreement set the tone for what followed. It began with the assertion that Britain should play a 'leading role' in an 'enlarged' European Union, a strikingly arrogant and self-delusory formulation. As long as Britain continues to be the semi-detached member of the European Union which psychologically and institutionally it has become in recent years, all thoughts of British 'leadership' in the European Union are fantasy. Moreover, as even a cursory acquaintance with the subject would show, the question of further enlargement of the European Union is a highly controversial one throughout the Union. It is not even insularity, it is simple solipsism to imagine that a bald assertion of its desirability by the British government can make it occur. The enlargement of the European Union is not a subject on which our partners are waiting for British leadership.

Nor will Britain's partners have derived much encouragement to take seriously British views on the future of the Union, regarding enlargement or anything else, from the remaining lines of the agreement's introductory paragraph. The new government did not believe that any 'further powers should be transferred to Brussels without a referendum' and argued that the general European policy of the Coalition should be to strike a balance between 'constructive engagement with the EU' and 'protecting our national sovereignty'.

The wilful misrepresentation of the European Union as an entity entirely separate from its member states, a polity which has its sinister lair in 'Brussels,' is familiar but absurd in British political rhetoric. It entirely misdescribes the nature of the European Union, which is a political organisation based on reciprocal sovereignty-pooling. Power is shared by the United Kingdom with Berlin, Madrid and Warsaw or any other of the national capitals, not with the Commission in Brussels, just as the Germans, Spanish and others share it with London. To elevate the protection of 'our national sovereignty' to a specific goal of European policy is a disavowal of the fundamental principles upon which the European Union is constructed. Those who depict the Union simply as a process of 'ceding' or 'transferring' or even 'losing' British sovereignty are guilty either of intellectual laziness or political chicanery. In the latter case, their conscious or unconscious goal is to instil a negative and unattractive image of the Union's workings in the mind of their listeners.

A similar effect arises from the appalling phrase 'constructive engagement' in the Coalition agreement - one not made any more acceptable through its occasional use by the New Labour government. 'Constructive engagement' is a term used by diplomats and others to signify their distaste for a government with which they are in negotiation, such as Iran, Korea or South Africa in the era of apartheid. For any political party to see it as an appropriate description of Britain's dealings with its closest partners in the European Union, with whom we have voluntarily decided to share important elements of our national sovereignty, is breathtaking. Even more astounding is the juxtaposition of 'constructive engagement' and 'preserving our national sovereignty'. It seems that 'constructive engagement' was to be the positive side of the Coalition's European policy. For those who have a genuinely favourable, even enthusiastic view of Britain's role in the European Union, 'constructive engagement' will be as good as it gets over the five envisaged years of the Coalition government.

-o0o-

Those hoping (and hope springs eternal in the breast of most Euro-enthusiasts) that the body of the Coalition agreement would be less sour in tone than the introductory summary should have been sorely disappointed as they read on. The first paragraph of the main text paid lip-service to the concept of Britain's being a 'positive participant' in the Union, playing a 'strong and positive role with our partners' in pursuit of the bizarrely limited agenda which the Coalition agreement conceded, not apparently to the Union, but to the 'nations of Europe', namely global competitiveness, global warming and global poverty.

There was no reference here to strengthening Europe's voice in the world, economic co-ordination, human rights in Europe or elsewhere, immigration or internal security. Yet these are the issues that will dominate the agenda of the European Union over the next decades. The Coalition government will need to find a better response to these European topics rather than to wish that they did not exist. The hope that it will be possible for the Coalition government to be seen as a 'positive participant' on the basis of its reductionist agenda is wholly unconvincing.

More emphatic, on the other hand, as a statement of the Coalition's aspirations is the long list of negative policies to which it committed itself. There would be no 'further transfer of sovereignty or powers over the course of the next Parliament' and the Coalition would also examine the 'balance of the EU's existing competencies', working in particular to 'limit the application of the Working Time Directive in the United Kingdom'. The first of these commitments is purely ideological in character, since it is impossible to predict whether over that period it would or would not be in the national interest to engage in further sovereignty-pooling through the European Union. If the second means anything, it will presumably mean junior doctors working longer hours, hardly a demonstration of the supposed superiority of British over European decision-making.

But it was with the promise to introduce a referendum bill on future European treaties that the Coalition agreement nailed its colours to the Eurosceptic mast before which so many of its supporters sail. The terms in which this policy is described are illuminating. It is no surprise that the Conservative Party should envisage future potential European treaties as simply implying further 'transferred areas of power'. It is more depressing that its Liberal Democrat partners should have acquiesced in this. Perhaps the most striking phrase of the agreement was that used to describe the referendum bill as a 'lock'. This made it obvious that the agreement's signatories have little interest in the holding of European referendums for their own sake, as exercises in participatory democracy, but see them only as instruments to constrain future British participation in European integration.

The Conservative Party is hardly known for favouring referendums. Mrs Thatcher herself liked to quote the description of them as 'instruments of dictatorship'. No such qualms beset her successors when they think they see an opportunity to put a spoke in the wheel of European integration. As a conscious expression of its fundamental Euroscepticism, the Coalition wants to ensure that a future British government will be constrained from signing a European treaty in the national interest because any referendum on the subject would be impossible to win in the face of ruthless and well-funded opposition from dubious interest groups and their friends in the media. The political and philosophical arguments against referendums on treaties are well-known: if representative democratic assemblies have any central task of scrutiny to perform, it ought to be precisely in this field of complicated compromises and delicate balancing of interests that international treaties presuppose.

In the case of the proposed referendum bill for future European treaties, there is a further intellectual dishonesty from its advocates, which first came to light in September 2010, when David Lidington, the European Minister, set out in greater detail the likely contents of the EU Bill to a Parliamentary Committee. From his remarks, it was clear that the Coalition intended to exempt accession treaties from the need for a national referendum in the United Kingdom. This was either intellectual laziness or dishonesty. If it makes sense for a referendum to be held on the question of whether a further part of British sovereignty should be shared within the existing European Union, it makes much more sense for one to take place on the sharing of those many aspects of British sovereignty already pooled in the European Union with such potential new members of the Union as Croatia or Turkey.

When a new country joins the European Union, it acquires for itself a say in the exercise of a portion of British sovereignty. There can be no logical justification for the withholding of a national referendum on that issue by those who favour such a referendum on any other European treaty. The refusal to envisage referendums on enlargement (which the Conservative Party, largely for unavowed reasons, favours) stands in flagrant contrast with the desire to ensure that any other European treaty will be subjected to a 'referendum lock'. Before the committee, Mr. Lidington argued that accession treaties took place exclusively between the acceding country and 'the European Union', as if the United Kingdom were not a component part of the Union. This wilful misconception throws a flood of light on the thinking of the new government about European issues.

Another central commitment of the Coalition agreement was that Britain will not join or prepare to join the euro in the current Parliament. There is much justified criticism to be made of the last Labour government's approach to the euro. Internal division within the government and lack of political direction on this issue ensured that over thirteen years the economic and political case for British membership of the euro went by default. But not even Mr. Brown in his most surly moments would have considered taking such an irrevocably marginalising step for Britain within the European Union as to rule out British membership of the euro for well over five years, and probably effectively for ten. The authors of the Coalition agreement well understood what they were doing in stipulating that no preparations for joining the euro should be made in this Parliament. Any new government would require most of its period in office to lay the political and economic groundwork for British membership of the single European currency.

Over the coming months and years, the institutional structures of the single European currency will be reformed in a way at least as important as was their original design. If Britain had been a country unsure about whether and in what circumstances it would join the euro, as it was under successive New Labour governments, its influence on this process of reform would have been limited. Now that the Coalition government has declared its hand on this matter so clearly, with the Conservatives being against British membership in any circumstances and the Liberal Democrats prepared to accept a delay of at least seven years, British influence on this question has become non-existent. Yet Britain joined the European Community in 1973 not least to exert appropriate influence within its decision-making fora on matters likely to be of vital concern to the United Kingdom.

The political culture of 'opt-outs', 'red lines' and of special arrangements for the United Kingdom, pursued with increasing vigour by New Labour over the past thirteen years, did much to reduce British influence within the European Union. The Coalition government's agreed policy on the euro could only be a prelude to the continuation of that baleful process. The Coalition agreement gives a clear warning that the predominant tone of its European policy will be one of obstruction and standing aside as far as possible from the future development of the European Union. The concluding paragraphs of the Coalition agreement's provisions on Europe, promising a 'strong [defence] of the UK's national interest' in the forthcoming negotiations on the European budget; calling for a single seat for the European Parliament; rejecting British participation in the establishment of any European public prosecutor; and renewing the British government's commitment to enlargement faithfully echo the sour and negative tone of the early portion of the text.

Only in regard to the Coalition's approach to questions of criminal justice was a marginally different tone struck by the agreement. In this area, the Coalition would judge issues on a case-by-case basis 'with a view to maximising our country's security'. That the Conservative Party will not always put its anti-European obsession before 'our country's security' is of course to be welcomed. That it should seem pleasantly surprising says much about the depth of this Conservative anti-European obsession in recent years.

An argument often heard from those on the broadly pro-European side of British politics who supported the Coalition agreement, including its provisions on European policy, was that the negative rhetoric on European topics was simply preparing the way for a pragmatic retreat from the Conservative Party's more radical anti-European posturing when it was in opposition; and that in any case a new European treaty in the near future which would trigger an unpredictable British referendum is unlikely, still less Britain's being able or willing to join the euro in the foreseeable future. On this analysis, the appearance of concessions on European issues by the Liberal Democrats to the Conservative Party was much greater than the reality. If at some point in the medium term future, the economic case for joining the euro suddenly became overwhelming, the Conservative Party in government would no doubt adjust its attitudes accordingly. Should an unexpectedly compelling reason for a new European treaty occur in the next five years, it would be for the government of the day to find reasons why a referendum need not be held on the text in question, or devote all its efforts to winning the referendum.

Over the past twenty years, pro-Europeans of all political parties in the United Kingdom have comforted themselves with a series of delusions, such as that the

Conservative Party would rapidly emancipate itself from the infantile disorder of Euroscepticism; that the New Labour government was working quietly behind the scenes to facilitate British entry into the euro; that Mr. Blair would triumphantly win a referendum on the Constitutional Treaty; that the Conservative Party in government would pursue a more pragmatic European policy than its electoral rhetoric might suggest.

The common thread of all these delusions has been the complacent assumption that history and events were ineluctably moving in the pro-European direction. There would come a time, perhaps in the context of a referendum supported by all the great and good, when the pro-European forces would need to rally and assert themselves. Until then, pro-Europeans could afford to view with lofty indifference the vulgarities of radical Euroscepticism. Any pro-European 'crusading' to counter that of the Eurosceptics was unnecessary, inappropriate and unwelcome, for differing reasons, to pro-Europeans from all the main political parties.

The outcome of this complacency and cowardice has been that over the past twenty years, pro-Europeanism in this country has declined from being the intellectual mainstream of political discourse in this country to a distinctly minority position, and not infrequently a persecuted one at that. All too often, the political and public debate now seems to revolve only around the degree of suspicion or hostility towards the European Union - essentially whether semi-detachment or final estrangement is the best course for our country. The Coalition agreement falls squarely into this category of debate, adopting the view that Britain should not leave the European Union, but should treat with the greatest possible degree of suspicion any deeper participation in its structures.

There is a temptation, when the political environment is unpropitious, to pursue a minimalist agenda, congratulating oneself on small victories achieved and major disasters averted. There seems a persuasive rationale for arguing that British semi-detachment from the European Union, even if extended over many years to come, is less damaging to British interests than is withdrawal from the Union. But two important considerations speak against any such approach, one of experience and the other of logic. First, the pursuit by the once numerous pro-Europeans of this country of a minimalist agenda, through complacency first and now through resignation, has contributed to the rampant successes of Euroscepticism over the past decades. The quiet satisfaction of some who regard themselves as pro-European with the terms of the Coalition agreement was entirely of a piece with this attitude. The European Council of December 2011 should have demonstrated beyond any doubt, reasonable or otherwise, just how misplaced this satisfaction was.

Second, pro-Europeans in this country need to fear for the future. There is no logical reason why the European semi-detachment that underwrites the Coalition agreement should be the end of Britain's movement away from the European Union. The view of the Union implicit in that agreement is one which could well lead in the medium term to the natural conclusion that Britain has no place in the European Union. When such central values of the Union as sovereignty-sharing, community of interest and joint institutions mean so little to the British government, the question will pose itself with increasing urgency, just why does it believe that Britain should continue being a member of a Union, apparently hell-bent, as its major political project, on depriving all European nations of their sovereignty and national identity?

The authors of this book firmly believe that Britain would be better served by a fuller participation in the European Union, rather than self-torturing agonising about its degree of marginalisation. We explicitly favour wholehearted (rather than merely 'constructive') engagement in (and not 'with') the European Union. Those who share that view are no doubt a minority within the United Kingdom at the moment. But minorities and majorities are apt to change with time, as the recent history of this country shows. Our hope is that the minority who already agree with us may benefit from having their sometimes inchoate views articulated vigorously and publicly - and that thus encouraged, the minority may begin the long fight to become a majority once more. There are advantages to being comfortably in the political Eurosceptic mainstream in this country. This book is the attempt of its authors to suggest that there is political challenge and intellectual coherence to be found outside that comfortable self-indulgence.

Chapter Two: The Conservatives:
The long road from Euro-enthusiasm

Since the demise of Edward Heath's accident-prone government in 1974 we can, with dismay and disbelief, look back on more than three decades of self-delusion from British ministers and members of the Conservative Party at all levels of the hierarchy. A saga of revisionism, double dealing with our EU partners, and nationalistic post-imperial arrogance on a grand scale, remains a sad commentary on how this country has missed every important European bus by being, on a constant basis, a bad, unenthusiastic member of the club.

At least John Major managed in the end, despite the buffeting from large numbers of his own colleagues, to get the Maastricht Treaty through Parliament (indeed without a referendum) with a tiny vote and a ludicrous commitment – for a so-called proud sovereign country – to await the results from the Danish referendum before ratification! Thereafter he showed some dignity and was courageous enough to make sure he resubmitted himself for election as party leader. Tragically however he did not change his behavioural weaknesses towards the 'bastards', as he himself called them. He woefully failed to move away from the constant obsession with appeasing the unappeasable. He was urged repeatedly to change this fatal style. He was still afraid of his Eurosceptic colleagues, despite many pleas. No wonder John Major lost to Labour and Tony Blair in the biggest ever post-war loss of his own colleagues' seats, Conservative constituencies falling like ninepins.

John Major's blunders were not the only problem. The original fault lay in his predecessor's almost psychotic loathing of the European Community, which got worse and worse after her second election victory. Mrs Thatcher seemed to take a perverse pleasure in causing unnecessary rows in the Council of Ministers on numerous occasions. These should be remembered as object lessons in how not to behave in a community of like-minded nations working for the common good. No wonder sensible politicians like Germany's Chancellor Helmut Schmidt, France's President Giscard d'Estaing and Italy's Prime Minister Giulio Andreotti could barely listen to the nationalist venom dressed up as policy from this self-important politician. In the end, on many such occasions, she was forced to give way, in view of the obvious commonsense of the proposals actually on the table.

All this was a far cry from the heady and exciting days when Prime Minister Heath had, after long discussions, persuaded a puzzled French President Georges Pompidou that the British really were a full-hearted European nation.

Ted Heath made many mistakes in his four years at Number 10. But in the end he did much good for Britain by overcoming legitimate French objections. His friends were always particularly impressed too by his wisdom in two respects, apart from his attractive European attitudes. Firstly, he had a deep scepticism of the ability of modern US politicians to create intelligent foreign policy decisions. Secondly, he had a healthy reserve about the quality of secret services in all countries, including our own. In the US case of course these two explosive weaknesses came together in a lethal cocktail of foreign policy incompetence after Eisenhower and Kennedy.

Mercifully the positive Europeans in Britain realised that counterweights to this transatlantic foolishness were needed urgently, both in the step-by-step development of a common European foreign policy, and in a coherent Western response to the new major superpowers coming up. For the Conservative Parliamentary Party, the Heath effect failed to ensure a continuity of enthusiasm for the then EEC, since his two election defeats in 1974 made him very unpopular amongst more and more colleagues. The need for cross-party support for the entry terms unfortunately also created a culture of House of Commons committees designed to 'keep the European Community at bay', a culture based on wholly negative motives rather than the more genuine desire for scrutiny that can be seen nowadays, especially in the Lords.

Side by side with these woeful trends there sprang up the culture of being generally more anti-European for political parties in opposition. This was a depressing phenomenon not witnessed in any of the other member states before the enlargement of 2004. The one exception to this rule occurred in 1975, when for many Conservatives in opposition being opposed to Harold Wilson was more important to them than their underlying feelings about Europe. Thatcher and other right-wingers campaigned vigorously for a yes vote in the controversial referendum, reflecting the eight to one vote for the newly renegotiated terms at the previous Tory conference - heady days indeed.

Thereafter it was downhill all the way once Edward Heath had been despatched in favour of the "Dame de Fer". The country witnessed a period of lukewarm attitudes towards Europe by the intervening Callaghan government (which tried to postpone the first EP elections) until the Thatcherite hatred of Europeans – 'they are so weak' – truly came into its own. From the drama of the entry legislation under Ted Heath, when Liberal MPs as well as Roy Jenkins' famous group of 68 saved the embattled premier on numerous notable occasions, Tory long-term sourness towards Europe began in the 1980s to develop its slow poison.

Other Community member states, especially Holland, France, Germany and Luxembourg remained deeply shocked that any British government was prepared to use renegotiation as a regular tool to remind these misguided continentals that Britain was still a world power with close links to the USA and a historically significant Commonwealth. Britain's deteriorating trading performance and poor management in manufacturing paradoxically made successive British governments ever more myopic and defiant in the face of all the empirical evidence.

Mrs Thatcher espoused the merits of young businessmen driving their own Jaguars by the age of 29, whilst forgetting that the greatest output triumph of Jaguar – before it was rescued by more competent foreign management – was to reach a mere 36,000 cars annually under John Eagan. We recall also the excited, young Tory Macmillanite pro-European MP proudly announcing in the tearoom that President Mitterrand had sent him an invitation to the 14th July parade in Paris. One purple-faced elderly colleague exploded in response that it was wrong to attend because our chaps were the finest marchers in the world. When Giscard d'Estaing was asked by his cabinet adviser what he thought of Mrs Thatcher, he was reputed to have replied: 'Je ne l'aime, ni comme homme, ni comme femme.'

However it was the anti-German stance of the Tory Iron Lady and her acolytes that particularly upset both the Germans and their new friends in post-war Europe. Franco-German reconciliation led by Konrad Adenauer and François-Poncet – as first French Ambassador to the new republic – was the greatest story ever of the new European recovery (and a good lesson to the Israelis and Palestinians in a different context). Mrs Thatcher would not take any of it. For her, the Germans were definitely strange and different. They were up to mischief if they could get away with it. But what was unbearable was that they were successful, even at modern capitalism, on a scale the British could only dream about. They should have understood that Britain was a leading country in the world, not a mere European power. To Mrs Thatcher, the Germans seemed to fly in the face of her own brand of common sense, with strong trade unions also serving on companies' second boards and very limited privatisation after careful cross-party consultation. The Germans had massive manufacturing prowess but also emerging new financial services like banking and insurance. They had coalitions of moderate people, huge exports, a strong currency and at the same time a willingness by the political classes to give this currency up for the sake of European unity – a quite amazing phenomenon.

When Harold Wilson's crude attempts to keep his own party together did allow the pro-Europe Labourites to work with the Tories, there was the beginning of a possible bi-partisanship (the Liberals being strongly Europhile anyway) which has usually been a feature of domestic European policy in most member states of the Union. In France all the parties traditionally worked closely together on these issues (including much later the single currency) except for the backward National Front and the Communist Party. Although initially Mrs Thatcher behaved reasonably in line with her enthusiasm for a yes vote in the 1975 referendum, this soon gave way to her tendency to distance herself from too much contamination by European thinking and her quiet encouragement of nationalistic right-wing colleagues, like Angus Maude and Airey Neave. Mrs Thatcher's obsession with America continued apace, even though our EEC allies deserved better from their willingness to concede a special budget rebate for the UK.

The budgetary controversy turned into one of the most depressing examples of British intransigence and enforced acrimony towards an ever-patient Council of Ministers. Finally, when Lord Carrington managed at last after almost four years of trouble and strife to obtain in 1982 a huge reduction in Britain's net contribution to the European budget, the only country to secure at the time such an exceptional agreement, his own leader was angry and recalcitrant. But it was hardly the fault of our continental partners that our lower farm output and different pattern of imports from outside the EC imposed an artificially large net European budgetary payment on the UK. If Britain had accepted the original invitation to be a founder member of the European Community, it would have been possible to create a somewhat different CAP. Having been conceded as a temporary measure, the special UK rebate lasted some twenty years until Blair was forced to surrender 25 per cent of it in 2005. As we have remained a low-output, excessively importing country, the rebate has assumed extra importance for the British economy.

At least, after initial hostility, Mrs Thatcher embraced the Single European Act in 1986 – thinking it was simply a matter of promoting free trade. At the same time she rejected much of what was implied by the Act – including future monetary union. Her previously right-wing anti-Europe Commissioner, Arthur Cockfield, had by the time of the Act converted to a fervent pro-Europeanism. Indeed all the Eurosceptic politicians from Britain from both parties seconded to Europe rapidly 'went native' for self-evident reasons. Britain's partners thought that the SEA and the concession of the British budget rebate, as well as a gradual learning curve, would change Margaret Thatcher's attitudes. She however maintained her frenzied, but ultimately unsuccessful resistance to plans for monetary union, including the pre-euro exchange rate mechanism, which even her own docile ministers had insisted on joining. Another leading Conservative supporting Mrs Thatcher in her opposition of the Exchange Rate Mechanism was Norman Lamont, whose later tenure as Chancellor of the Exchequer was so inglorious.

If John Major had been braver in facing down his poisonous and growing band of Eurosceptic rebels, arguably he might have mitigated the subsequent Labour triumph in 1997. It must anyway not be forgotten that an electoral 'triumph' for a sole party under our voting system is worth less than the real majority demanded by virtually all other member states, except France. Most other EU members regard the British national election system as little short of a breach of human rights! Looking back, we can see that it was a great tragedy for Britain, and for the Conservatives themselves, that they became the little-Englander-cum-US-colony-party under the most narrow-minded Prime Minister in history. The damage done persists to this day. Without the constant repair work of the Foreign Office the harm done would have been even worse.

As the late David Watt wrote in the press on one of Patrick Cosgrave's flattering books about Mrs Thatcher, the author did at least end up making her famous dynamism and obsession seem both human and dotty. What a pity that this dynamism was not devoted more to enhancing our role in Europe. It could then have been a very different story, one of vindicating President Pompidou's assurances to his fellow founder member states that this time Britain had changed from international geo-political pomposity to reality at last. It would have been possible to refute General de Gaulle's claim in 1963 that Britain was the enduring lackey of US foreign policy.

-o0o-

In 1997 Tony Blair took over in a vast wave of political euphoria never before seen in post-war Britain – at least since the sensational Attlee win in 1945. This was followed by a series of retreats from settled policies for the dazed Tory Party, especially on European policy. A depressing succession of failed leaders, William Hague, Iain Duncan Smith and Michael Howard succeeded in keeping their party in a prolonged wilderness, not least because they thought that hatred of all things European was synonymous with the future revival of their own tattered party. A small number of increasingly besieged pro-Europeans struggled on bravely, with some leading figures such a Michael Heseltine and Ken Clarke standing up, at least initially, strongly for important European objectives, above all for joining the euro. The Lion and the Bruiser even rashly attended Blair's fraudulent Imax launch of the Britain in Europe campaign, which, by design, exactly coincided with the eclipse of the once proud and bold European Movement.

With William Hague suggesting in 2001 that ten days remained to 'save the pound', Iain Duncan Smith ruling out joining the euro forever, and Michael Howard showing similar attitudes, the pro-European impetus in the Tory Party was finally dissolved, both wilfully and by negligence. This was the culmination of a sequence of squalid and incompetent developments for a party that fortunately can no longer govern on its own. When the new Coalition government came into being in May 2010, some commentators expected that the presence of the Liberal Democrats in office might serve to soften the most extreme manifestations of Conservative hostility to the European Union. In the first year of the Coalition, this sometimes appeared a realistic expectation. Events however in the last quarter of 2011 have taken a very different turn, with the Prime Minister clearly shaken by the substantial revolt of the Conservative backbenches in October 2011, at the heart of which lay the European issue. His response to this could be seen in his counter-productive tactics during and after the European Council of early December last year. Having failed to protect, if they needed protecting, the interests of the City of London and having made more difficult the resolution of the Eurozone crisis, a resolution for which he has long been calling, Mr. Cameron was hailed by his uncritical anti-European backbenchers as a hero for his isolation in the European Council. These events mark an important new stage in Conservative policy towards the European Union. Conservative commitment to leaving the European Union in the foreseeable future can no longer be ruled out. The combination of a Prime Minister obsessed with party management and a party obsessed with the supposed iniquities of the European Union is a combination which promises nothing positive for Britain's position in Europe over the coming years.

Chapter Three:
Labour: From honest division to cynicism

The British political system was profoundly changed in the 1990s, at least for the short term, by the election to the Labour leadership of Tony Blair and his pursuit of the revisionist politics known as 'New Labour'. Mr. Blair believed that the Labour Party which he had inherited was destroying its electoral prospects by allowing British voters to associate the party with a number of unpopular policies and attitudes, such as punitive tax rates, poor management of the economy, commitment to wide public ownership in crucial areas of the economy and excessive tolerance of law-breaking. To some extent, Mr. Blair's predecessor as Labour leader, John Smith, had shared this analysis and worked to 'modernise' the policies of the party until his sudden death in 1994. But the decade during which Mr. Blair led the Labour Party saw an acceleration and generalisation of this process, which it is difficult to imagine his predecessor would have wished to execute.

European policy played some role in this radical remodelling of the Labour Party, particularly in the early years of the Labour government elected in 1997. But New Labour's European policy should not be viewed as something distinct from the general political and electoral matrix from which New Labour sprang – it was intended to help the party win the election. The EU has never been a high priority for Labour. Far from being a pro-European party, a more accurate description might be that New Labour found it electorally advantageous to present itself as an 'anti-anti-European' party.

Since the 1960s, Europe has been a controversial question within the Labour Party, and for much of that period the party saw itself as politically hostile to the European Community. It was a Labour leader, Hugh Gaitskell, who in 1960 warned melodramatically against abandoning one thousand years of British history. When Britain signed the Treaty of Rome in 1972, only a minority of Labour Members of Parliament supported Edward Heath's government in that decision. The Labour government elected in 1974 was deeply divided on the question of continuing British membership of the Community. After a limited renegotiation of the terms of British membership, the Labour Prime Minister Harold Wilson put the results of that renegotiation to a referendum in 1975. In a unique reversal of British constitutional practice, serving members of the Labour cabinet of the day were allowed during the referendum campaign to argue for a rejection of their own government's renegotiated terms of membership.

In the event, the referendum produced a substantial majority in favour of continued British membership of the Community and the Labour governments of Harold Wilson and James Callaghan pursued until 1979 a European policy reflecting, albeit without any great enthusiasm, this clear-cut result. Ironically, in view of later events, Mr. Wilson and Mr. Callaghan were criticised by the Conservative opposition for their unenthusiastic approach to European issues. Nobody who voted Conservative in the General Election of 1979 will have done so because he or she wished for a more restrictive or sceptical approach to British membership of the European Community.

As the Labour Party moved to the left in the early 1980s, so the coldness towards the Community which it had shown in government turned into institutional hostility. Labour spokesmen liked at this time to claim that the Community's core values of free trade and political integration would prevent the implementation of genuinely socialist policies in the United Kingdom by any future Labour government. In the General Election of 1983, the Labour manifesto called for withdrawal from the Community. In the General Election of 1987, the party stopped short of calling for withdrawal, but could not hide its distrust of and distaste for the Community. Many later leading figures in New Labour fought in the elections of 1983 and 1987 without disavowing their party's manifesto at the time.

It was only in the late 1980s that the well-entrenched hostility of the Labour Party towards the European Community began to soften, partly in response to a widely-reported speech given by Jacques Delors to the British

Trade Union Congress in 1988. In this speech, Mr. Delors claimed that the Community had much to offer the British Labour movement in the way of new social legislation. His claim greatly pleased his audience, but had greatly exaggerated the capacity of the European Community to change national social policy. Yet his words fuelled the growing hostility to the European Community of the then British Prime Minister, Margaret Thatcher. Mr. Delors no doubt simply wished to make a helpful intervention in British political discussion, encouraging the left of British politics to take a more positive view of the European Community. The paradoxical outcome of his speech, however, was to reinforce the growing alienation of the traditionally pro-European British right, while cultivating only very shallow-rooted and opportunistic pro-Europeanism within the Labour Party and its affiliates.

In 1992, John Smith (who in 1972 had voted for British membership of the European Community), became leader of the Labour Party. His leadership saw an improvement in relations between the Labour Party and other left-wing parties in continental Europe, almost all of whom, with the exception of some national Communist parties, were enthusiastic supporters of deeper European integration. Even so, when the Conservative Party found itself divided in the early 1990s on the question of the ratification of the Maastricht Treaty, Prime Minister John Major received little help from Mr. Smith's Parliamentary Labour Party. The adversarial and tribal nature of British politics makes it tempting for large political parties to exploit the divisions of their opponents, almost irrespective of any wider political context. The Conservative Party emerged from its traumatic debates on the Maastricht Treaty divided and weakened in its traditional pro-European attitudes. The torch of pro-Europeanism has only fitfully been taken up by the Labour Party over the past twenty years. If John Smith had lived longer, another, more principled course might have been possible for Labour's European policy. As events fell out, his legacy on European issues can only be regarded as a mixed one.

When Tony Blair became leader in 1994, he concluded that one of the elements which needed to be abandoned in the remodelled Labour Party was its anti-Europeanism. But this was not unconditional. Electoral calculation was at the heart of New Labour's approach: unreflective hostility to Europe was in Mr. Blair's view part of the package of 'Old Labour' attitudes, unacceptable to the middle class voters whom New Labour was now attempting to woo. A significant tranche of these latter voters was coming to be repelled by the growing shrillness with which the European question was debated within the Conservative Party. It was good party politics to remind such electors that New Labour now rejected old-fashioned nationalism, whether of the Old Labour or modern Conservative variety. This analysis underlay Mr. Blair's ambiguous approach to the single European currency in the mid-1990s and beyond.

In the months before the General Election of 1997, the Labour Party was demonstrably pursuing a double tactic in what it said about British membership of the euro. Its strategists were generally convinced that Labour would benefit electorally from the abandonment of reflexive anti-Europeanism, but those same strategists were eager to pre-empt accusations of uncritical acceptance of every proposal emanating from the European Union. Mr. Blair therefore adopted before the General Election of 1997 the Conservative government's pledge to hold a referendum before taking Britain into the euro. Shortly before the Election itself he published an article in the notoriously Eurosceptic newspaper the 'Sun' telling its readers about how much he 'loved' the pound. New Labour's 'love affair' with the European Union and specifically with the euro was from the beginning a relationship of calculated self-advantage rather than one of passionate conviction.

New Labour's politically opportunistic view of the single European currency could be seen early in the new government's term in office. That minority of New Labour ministers genuinely eager for Britain rapidly to join the euro hoped that the newly-elected government would use some of its immense political capital shortly after the General Election to hold and win a referendum on the principle of joining the euro. Instead, after a confused set of discussions between the Prime Minister and his chancellor, Gordon Brown, the new government adopted a set of five criteria (economic convergence, employment, outside investment, impact on the City, economic flexibility) which it would apply in the coming years to judge whether it was to Britain's economic advantage to join the euro, and only recommend British membership of the single currency if and when these criteria were met. The decisive role of the present shadow Chancellor of the Exchequer, Ed Balls, in the haphazard formulation of these criteria was widely recognised at the time.

Formally, the five criteria remained throughout its period in office the basis of the government's approach to British membership of the single currency. An interim assessment of them was made in 2003, which concluded that the criteria had not yet been met. Apparently the tone and terms of this assessment were matters of long and acrimonious discussion between the Prime Minister and his Chancellor. Immediately after the assessment was completed, some commentators claimed that its contents opened the way for a relatively speedy entry into the single currency by the United Kingdom. Later remarks by the Chancellor and the Prime Minister showed how little substance there was in these hopes.

Mr. Blair in particular regularly presented the position of his government as equidistant between two misconceived and extremist attitudes, represented respectively by the Conservative Party and the Liberal Democrats. For Mr. Blair, the Conservatives were in error through their refusal ever to join the single currency, even if it was economically advantageous to do so; the Liberal Democrats were in error by advocating membership of the euro in circumstances that might be contrary to Britain's economic interests. For his government, the Prime Minister insisted, the matter was a pragmatic decision to be taken in the light of evolving economic circumstances. This was a view well attuned to British public sentiment in the late 1990s, when the euro was first set up. The British electorate was clearly uneasy at the prospect of ruling out membership of the single currency forever, but deeply hesitant before taking the decisive step of engaging further in European monetary and political integration through membership of the Eurozone. New Labour's Janus-like commitment to the five 'criteria' for euro membership was a successful 'triangulation' between the contrasting views of its political opponents, which faithfully mirrored the uncertain attitude of the British electorate.

It has often been claimed that Mr. Blair was emotionally more committed to Britain's eventual membership of the euro than was his Chancellor, and that Mr. Brown in his turn used the issue of the single currency as a weapon in his joust with Mr. Blair to ensure his early succession to the premiership. There is good reason to believe both these claims. New Labour's approach to the European single currency was a matter not merely of political positioning by the Labour Party, but also of political positioning within the Labour Party. As the custodian of the five 'criteria', Mr. Brown was able to stress his own independence of the Prime Minister by thwarting any desire of the latter to declare the 'criteria' met. Indeed, he went further, making more difficult the winning of any eventual referendum on the euro by his frequent and well-advertised diatribes against the European Commission, the supposed economic inflexibility of Britain's neighbours and the iniquities of the European budget.

The Prime Minister was unable to mobilise the determination or perhaps even the political capacity to overrule his Chancellor. No doubt many of his advisers were counselling him that a rupture with the Chancellor over European issues was politically dangerous ground on which to provoke a conflict. The need to preserve the internal and external political equilibrium of New Labour took precedence in his calculations over any personal inclination he may have had to move to quick resolution of the single currency issue.

One frequently-voiced criticism of New Labour as a political philosophy was its supposedly reactive nature, its over-emphasis on following public opinion as determined by polling or focus groups. European policy was an excellent example of this phenomenon. On many occasions since 1997, press reports have claimed that the government, and the Prime Minister in particular, was resolved upon a systematic campaign to change increasingly hostile British attitudes towards the single currency. No such campaign was mounted or even seriously attempted. New Labour did not even try to win the argument in favour of British membership of the euro.

In the past decade, the political debate concerning British membership of the euro has revolved essentially around two poles - those hostile to membership in all circumstances and the government's position which could envisage, but would not seek to promote, Britain's joining. The first view was well-financed, favoured by important elements of the media, and supported by the official opposition. The second was only intermittently promoted by a divided government, which was at least as interested in exploiting the divisions of its Conservative opponents and scoring Parliamentary points as in securing British membership of the single currency. From the beginning, the New Labour government's commitment to the euro had been tentative, conditional and manipulative. It was unsurprising that in the contest of ideas with those who propagated a clear message against British membership of the Eurozone, the latter secured a clear victory.

With the demise of the European Constitution, which on occasion the Prime Minister seemed to regard as an opportunity to combat the Euroscepticism which flourished so vigorously under his leadership, interest by New Labour in the European Union seemed at an unprecedentedly low ebb. This disengagement was reinforced by the realisation of many in his government that winning a referendum on the Constitution in 2006 might well have been an impossible challenge. When, in order to deprive the Conservative Party of a tactical advantage in the European Elections of 2004, Jack Straw persuaded the Prime Minister to reverse tack and promise a referendum on the European Constitution, he was taking a definite risk. The success of that gamble, arising from the rejection of the Constitution in the French and Dutch referendums, could not be guaranteed to repeat itself in two or three years' time.

The disappearance of the European Constitution in its original form was not the end of the evolving process of European integration. In the single market, in matters of internal security, in monetary policy and even in foreign policy, an institutional and political momentum exists which is far from having run its course. Mechanisms already exist whereby Britain can, if it wishes, participate only partly or not at all in these developments. But the price of this semi-detachment is that for the foreseeable future the British government will be unable to secure for the United Kingdom (except perhaps in the fields of foreign policy and, probably, defence policy) any leading role in the scope and pace of further European integration.

This ambiguous position may well be an outcome with which the great majority of the British electorate are content to live indefinitely. But two unfavourable possibilities may arise: the continuing integration of the European Union without Britain could develop in a way inimical to British interests; or European integration without Britain may be so economically and politically successful that Britain will wish in ten years time to 'reconnect' with the European mainstream on terms less favourable than it might have achieved but for its hesitation.

It would be truly ironic if the government confronting this latter circumstance and the Prime Minister seeking to join the European single currency were Conservative. Until Mrs Thatcher it was the Conservative Party which in British politics was the primary advocate and initiator of Britain's whole-hearted membership in the European Community. The move towards radical Euroscepticism in that party, stopping only just short of calls for withdrawal from the Union, has created a new equilibrium (from the authors' point of view a disequilibrium) in British political discourse on the European Union. This may now seem a permanent element of the British political scene. Nothing, however, is permanent in democratic politics. Europe may well still have surprises in store for the British political parties and their leaders.

Chapter Four:
The Liberal Democrats lose their idealism

In this inevitably gloomy saga of British political attitudes towards Europe over the past thirty years, the one ray of light, at least until recently, has been the Liberal Democrats and their predecessor parties. Tory backsliding and Labour uncertainty towards the European Union found traditionally little sympathy among Liberal Democrat peers and MPs. The MPs and Liberal Democrat peers who made up the Liberal Democrat Parliamentary Party in 2001 saw their party's long-standing enthusiasm for British membership of the EU membership as simply a routine aspect of the party's range of main policies. Even if there were occasional hesitations of individual Liberal Democrat parliamentarians on specific items of European policy, and leading West Country MPs like Nick Harvey and John Burnett were sometimes reluctant to advertise their pro-

European convictions, the leaders of the party, from Paddy Ashdown to Charles Kennedy to Menzies Campbell, were noted for their passionate advocacy of the European cause. As late as 2005, Charles Kennedy was still calling enthusiastically for British adherence to the euro.

When the Lisbon Treaty Bill arrived for parliamentary scrutiny in 2008, there were however a number of amendments put down by Liberal Democrat MPs which had at least quasi-nationalistic undertones in their wording. In the Lords by contrast not a single Liberal Democrat amendment was put down. The Liberal Democrat team in the Lords worked closely with Cathy Ashton to bring the Bill through intact. At this time, debates at the spring and autumn conferences of the Liberal Democrats still reflected the long-standing support of the party rank-and-file for the European Community, with only a few eccentric exceptions. The rank-and-file were entirely at one with their parliamentary representatives who had participated so vigorously in the 1997 Britain in Europe campaign, initially encouraged but then abandoned by Tony Blair.

What distinguished the Liberal Democrat approach to Europe in the 1990s and the early years of this century was not merely general enthusiasm, or even keen adherence to certain main policy areas like the European social framework, overseas aid co-ordination, or indeed the euro itself. Liberal Democrats went much further than the other big parties on all aspects of integrationist policy. The attitudes surveys in Geddes and elsewhere in 1998 and 1999 definitely highlighted the party as the least sceptical on integration. Senior figures like Russell Johnston got warm support at party meetings for his repeated allusions to the subject.

The party fought the 1997 election campaign on a strong manifesto commitment to promote the UK as a country playing a leading role in 'shaping' European structures and democratising its institutions on a pan-European basis. The party's MEPs were notably in the forefront of public debate, forceful advocates of integration, only occasionally forced on the defensive by nationalism at home in the press and parliament. Philip Sherrington's piece in the British Journal of International Relations 2005 on political parties and the EU over 2000-2005 described the party as 'Europositive' in a way that needed no further emphasis.

During this period, Liberal Democrats were well aware that the UK's own repeated hesitations on aspects of important European policy formation would not have the effect of holding the others back from a project which had maintained its original momentum, not just among the founding six, but also among later joiners. Liberal Democrat spokesmen welcomed the European Constitutional Treaty as the next stage in the democratic and federal development of the Union. Robert Maclennan, a former Labour MP, but now a senior Liberal Democrat, was a particularly eloquent advocate of this view within the party. Most active Liberal Democrat members, both in parliament and outside, were for many years unequivocal in their advocacy of the EU's becoming a united, multi-member-state democracy with its own parliament rather than remaining a mere diplomatic club.

This support from the Liberal Democrat grassroots was reflected in an array of pro-European talent among their senior figures and elder statesmen. Notable in the early years were Jo Grimond and the outstanding Europhile, David Steel, both of them mirroring the stronger pro-

Europeanism always evident in Scotland and the Isles. Roy Jenkins preceded his distinguished contribution to the formation of the Social Democrats, and their subsequent merger in the Liberal Democrats, by his role as the first British President of the European Commission, from which post he launched the original plan for European monetary union in the early eighties. The only reasonable criticism that can be made of Lord Jenkins is he had too generous a view of Mr. Blair's good faith, not merely on European issues, but on changes in the British voting system as well. From the same generation came the equally distinguished name of Shirley Williams, who remains an undimmed and fervent European in all respects.

All this pro-European history of the Liberal Democrats sits oddly with the European attitudes of their present Coalition partner. Mr. Cameron may have tried in the early months of the Coalition to check the worst excesses of his colleagues with soothing bromides; but the stark facts of life within his own party remain. Before the 2010 election, Messrs Cameron and Hague wilfully whipped up their MPs' feelings by denouncing a wide range of EU policies and legislation, inveighing against the Lisbon Treaty and losing no occasion to rail against the supposedly wicked Brussels bureaucratic machine. Mr. Cameron's party left the centre-right grouping in the European Parliament, and under his leadership came to echo more and more the rhetoric of UKIP. After the General Election of 2010, the Conservative Party even sponsored the Europhobic Bill Cash MP as the new chairman of the Commons European Scrutiny Committee. The events surrounding the European Council of 2011 and the reaction they evoked in the Conservative Parliamentary Party should have surprised nobody.

Tragically, the isolationist posture of the Tories now seems likely to be imitated by a strange and unexpected metamorphosis amongst the junior partner of the new Coalition. This is not because of any visibly strong shift away from European enthusiasm amongst the general body of Liberal Democrat members. With supreme irony this change derives from a shift in attitudes among the leaders. Ever since Nick Clegg took over, the tone has begun to change. This shift has been reflected too in Vince Cable's intermittent scepticism about the single currency, and a number of other EU policy items. The fact that the leader and the industry secretary are now sounding an uncertain note on EU matters has not escaped the attention of their fellow Liberal Democrat MPs. There are many sitting Liberal Democrat MPs (not just in the South West) who are worried about their re-election. Many of them are apparently tempted to believe that Eurosceptic rhetoric will help their future political prospects.

In private, Nick Clegg has often referred scathingly to the friction and lack of co-ordination among the Brussels bureaucracy, a frustration perhaps deriving from his time in Leon Brittan's cabinet before becoming MEP for the East Midlands. In recent years, he has been more willing to publicise this discontent. This criticism has not always taken account of the objective difficulties inherent in blending different nations' civil service and parliamentary traditions into a single European model. Turf wars and lack of co-ordination in Brussels are often no worse than the intra-national problems seen inside a single country, as in the famous British battles between the British Treasury and other departments of state.

By far the unfairest outburst from Mr. Clegg came at the time of the parliamentary expenses scandal, when a small number of MPs of all parties stretched the existing vague rules too far in claiming various parliamentary expenses. Many MPs who had not done anything very wrong were driven out of politics by the hysteria that was stirred up by the three main party leaders competing for press approval and public support. At that stage Nick Clegg saw fit to make slighting reference to the 'Brussels gravy train', an astonishing remark for the leader of an avowed pro-EU party, and a clear sop to the anti-Europeans in general and the proprietors of the increasingly hysterical British press in particular.

The contrast between the radical courage and originality of Liberal Democrat European policy in the past, and the cultivation of pseudo-nationalist tendencies nowadays is a painful phenomenon It reinforces the public's developing euro-doubts as they see that Liberal Democrats in particular are no longer available to provide an antidote to the huge stream of poison pouring out of the general body politic on matters European. Even Paddy Ashdown was only able to praise the euro in the past tense in his Times article in November 2011, but he could not bring himself to advocate British membership of the single currency now. The Liberal Democrats once proudly stood up for the great cause of Europe. Now we see them crouching behind a totally negative Coalition deal, and flirting with growing Euroscepticism. It is very sad to see how Mr. Clegg and his colleagues have sold out their old fervour for a mess of ministerial pottage! When the Coalition splits, as split it must, there will be a window of opportunity for the Liberal Democrats to reassume their position as a leading pro-European party within the British body politic. There are still many within the ranks of the Liberal Democrats who are hoping for precisely that.

Chapter Five:
The federalist bogeyman

Other Europeans or Britons returning to the United Kingdom after a long period of living abroad are often shocked by the tone and content of British discussion about the European Union. There is a wilful and dogmatic ignorance underlying most of the debate, a resentment of any attempt to confront hysterical prejudice with facts or logic and an implicit assumption in the minds of most discussing the subject that any respect in which the European Union differs from British political practices is simply a further demonstration of the former's inferiority. These disagreeable and irrational attitudes are lovingly encouraged by idle and superficial national media, which are more properly to be regarded as propaganda and entertainment sheets rather than as serious contributors to public education. No similar situation can be found in any other member state of the European Union.

Nor is wilful ignorance about the European Union confined to the broad mass of the population who take little day-to-day interest in politics. This ignorance is widespread among the British political classes, even among those who profess themselves immune to the wilder fantasies of radical Euroscepticism. This lacuna ensures that defence, much less advocacy, of the European Union frequently passes by default in the United Kingdom. Those who supposedly favour a full role for Britain in the European Union often do not possess the knowledge or intellectual coherence of approach to allow them to give a robust and credible account of the nature of the Union and Britain's position within it.

It is easier for such tepid friends of the European Union in this country to accept, consciously or unconsciously, much of the Eurosceptic analysis. They argue only that the Union is probably not quite as bad as its most vitriolic critics assert, that it is changing in a way that will make it more acceptable to British Eurosceptics and that in any case Britain has no choice but to remain, albeit unenthusiastically, a member of the Union for fear of impotent isolation outside. It is hardly surprising that such lame and unpersuasive rhetoric makes little headway against the unbridled distortions of most presentations in the mass media of European questions.

Later chapters in this book will be devoted to specific areas of the European Union's policies, such as its budget, its Common Agricultural Policy, its external relations and the single European currency. All these are topics upon which grotesque misperceptions exist in British public and political opinion. But underlying all these sectoral questions, and indeed psychologically conditioning the British approach to them, is a deeper intellectual and moral confusion about the workings of the European Union, a confusion which again and again finds expression in a uniquely British bitterness and resentment towards the central European institutions. Successive democratically elected British governments have said for fifty years they wish Britain to be a member. Even today a majority of British voters claim in most opinion polls that they want their country to remain within the Union.

But this wish apparently co-exists in the minds of many British voters with the delusion that it is possible and desirable for the United Kingdom to be a member of the Union without participating in and being reciprocally affected by the Union's institutions. Many current British politicians also apparently share the belief that these are simply an optional extra which they can dismiss as they choose without thereby weakening fundamentally the case for the Union and Britain's role within it. But the European Union's institutions lie at its very core. Nor is their proper functioning conceivable without the whole-hearted contribution of the member states, such as Britain, to their success.

The systematic misrepresentation of these institutions and their interaction with the member states, including the United Kingdom, has been a major part of the propaganda against the European Union over the past twenty years in the United Kingdom. Central to the propaganda is the presentation of all the central European institutions as a single amorphous mass of unaccountable and intrusive bureaucrats. In fact, it is a defining characteristic of the European Union's system of governance that differing institutions, with differing roles and differing sources of legitimacy, offer a sophisticated and responsive political structure, in which power is deliberately dispersed. Caricatures of the Brussels monolith, intent on squeezing every last drop of national sovereignty out of the member states, are well wide of the mark, as even the most cursory review of the individual institutions will make clear.

–oOo–

No preconception is more illuminating of the refusal of much British opinion to understand the basic workings of the European Union than the sloppy but almost universal description of the European Commission as 'the civil service' of the Union. In most national administrations, civil servants are those who take instructions from their political masters, whether in the preparation of legislative proposals for national parliaments, or in the execution of administrative tasks entrusted to government by national legislatures. The Commission emphatically does not correspond to this political template, and because it does not, there frequently lurks beneath the surface the suspicion that the Commission is always illegitimately attempting to go beyond its proper role, seeking for itself prerogatives which properly belong to elected governments. The suspicion is ill-founded.

Far from taking instructions from national ministers, the Commission is explicitly charged by the European treaties to act independently of national governments, in the European interest. There have over the years been members of the European Commission over-eager to accept guidance, even instruction, from their national capitals. But far from acting in a way befitting their station as supposed simple functionaries, these individuals were flouting

the basic obligations of their offices. National governments nominate the European Commissioners who direct
the administrative and other activities of the Commission.
Once installed in their posts, however, these
Commissioners are called upon to exercise responsibilities
which logically cannot be discharged by messenger boys
from national capitals.

The two main responsibilities of the European
Commission are to propose and carry out, once adopted
by others, European legislation. It must be obvious that
neither of these tasks can be performed by a group of
twenty-seven national civil servants, all bound by instructions from their political masters. No legislative proposal
could possibly be the result of the unmediated clash
between apparently discordant national interests and traditions, with their constant vulnerability to sectional, regional and demagogic pressures. If it is to be in any way an
effective proposer of new European legislation, the
Commission must be able to act not merely as mediator,
but on occasion as arbiter between at least superficially
conflicting national positions.

Quite apart from the legal and moral constraints
imposed upon it by the treaties, the Commission could
not, as a matter of practicality, fulfil its task as proposer of
legislation if it saw itself as a body directly comparable to
the British civil service. There is no European government from which the European Commission could even
theoretically take instructions in its preparation of proposed new legislation. It would be interesting to know
how many of its critics would like to remedy this absence
by establishing a European government to which the
European Commission could be subordinated.

Almost more important than the role of independent proposer of new legislation is the role of the Commission as monitor and, together with the European Court of Justice, enforcer of adopted European legislation. Whenever European legislation is infringed, at least one national government is always directly or indirectly involved. For the Commission to be an effective monitor, it obviously needs to build up over time an autonomous position independent of national governments. In doing this, it is in no sense acting contrary to its allotted role within the European political system.

On the contrary, it is precisely fulfilling this role by its refusal to see itself as a mere secretariat for national governments. The European Union is founded on the proposition that decisions taken exclusively at the national level are not always the most rational, the most morally defensible or even the most economically advantageous to citizens of these national communities. The role of the European Commission in the structure of the Union is a reflection of this insight. Consciously or unconsciously, those in the United Kingdom who question the autonomy and legitimacy of the European Commission are questioning the founding principles of the European Union.

-oOo-

There also exists a pervasive impression in Britain that European legislation, binding upon the United Kingdom, is adopted in Brussels by a shadowy group of non-elected bureaucrats who then impose their diktats upon plucky but hapless democratic leaders in the member states. Nevertheless, to any observer not entirely given over to irrational prejudice against the European Union, the distinctive and central role of the Council of Ministers in the structure of the Union should surely provide reassurance that national politicians, interests and political cultures play a full and appropriate part in the way the Union functions.

If it is the role of the European Commission independently to provide proposals for European legislative initiatives, these proposals can never enter into law without the approval of the Council of Ministers and the European Parliament. Fulminations against the non-elected European Commission for its allegedly anti-democratic culture would be much more to the point if this were not the case. Within the European Union, all fundamental decisions are taken by democratically elected politicians, with their decision-making open to at least the same level of public scrutiny as in national political arenas. The role of national ministers meeting in the Council of Ministers to adopt legislation is particularly crucial. It is their decisions and those of the European Parliament that the European Commission is then called upon to execute. To this extent, and only to this extent, a legitimate parallel can be drawn between the Commission's role and that of national civil services.

Inherent in the Commission's function is that it cannot allow national governments to be sole judges of whether they are acting in accordance with the decisions of the Council of Ministers. This would be in effect to recognise the right of every government to evade the responsibilities arising from the decisions of the Council. Vast national resources are always available to national ministers to manufacture more or less plausible arguments about why their country cannot or should not implement decisions to which they were a prominent party. The vigilance of the

Commission is a bulwark against inevitable backsliding by national administrations who are often happier for their neighbours to carry out their European obligations than to do so themselves.

National governments have no excuses for such behaviour, as it is only in the very rarest cases that national governments have found themselves formally voted down by qualified majority voting in the Council. The members of the Council do their best to proceed by consensus, an attitude encouraged by the high threshold of acceptance set for decision-making, even where national vetoes are not formally available. The legislative and other decisions that issue from the Council represent the considered and carefully-arrived-at common decisions of twenty-seven democratically elected national governments, who then play a central part in implementing these decisions at home. To present this eminently reasonable, balanced and democratic method of decision-making as in any way dictatorial, invasive or megalomaniac is to fly in the face of the facts.

–o0o–

This structure of the European Union is further reinforced in its democratic credentials by the European Parliament, the directly elected representatives of voters throughout the Union. Since the first European Elections of 1979, the powers of the Parliament have regularly and substantially been increased, not primarily by its own actions, but by the national governments of the Union. These democratically elected national governments have concluded, rightly, that a more powerful Parliament makes for a more democratic and better-governed European

Union. Those who see the Union as simply the hollowing out of the member states of the Union to the advantage of overweening central institutions such as the Parliament will struggle to find any remotely plausible explanation for the apparent eagerness of member state governments to accelerate this process. The European Parliament is central to the democratic life of the Union. To deny as a matter of principle its capacity to fulfil this role is implicitly to reject a major component of the Union's political philosophy. It is becoming increasingly clear that many of the Parliament's critics in the United Kingdom do indeed want to do just that.

The European Union itself will probably never possess precisely similar structures to those of a member state of the Union. So the European Parliament cannot fairly be criticised or even praised because its competences and working methods are not precisely those of the House of Commons. Just as the latter have developed over time, so the role of the European Parliament may evolve in the coming decades, reflecting a deepening of integration which is the natural and wholly foreseeable path of development for the Union to assure its democratic legitimacy. Too many self-avowed pro-Europeans in this country find themselves on the wrong side of the argument about increasing the Parliament's powers.

The Parliament's most radical critics are not wrong when they say that European Elections would possess greater democratic legitimacy if they were fought on the basis of European-wide manifestos, by European-wide political parties and with demonstrable political consequences following from the results of those elections. Nor are they wrong in saying that the European Union suffers from the absence of a 'demos' like that of nation states, if by this they mean that there is at a popular level within the Union only a very fragmentary sense of a shared political identity. Some of the Union's defenders are inclined to underestimate the force of this critique, either because they take as axiomatic the democratic legitimacy of the directly-elected European Parliament, or because (as is often the case in this country) they do not anyway understand the crucial contribution the Parliament needs to be able to make to the democratic legitimisation of the Union.

Many arguments made by the Parliament's critics are of course opportunistic, designed to demonstrate the supposed impossibility of European democracy rather than to help bring it about. For them, European parliamentary democracy other than at the national level is simply inconceivable. Their contentions have recently received apparent support from a recent judgment of the German Constitutional Court, which casts considerable doubt upon the capacity of the European Parliament to act as an effective democratising component of the European Union. This latter judgment represents a change of view from earlier findings of the German Court, where the role of the European Parliament was much more positively assessed. There is no reason why its judgment should not change again. For this to happen, it will certainly be necessary and desirable to reform radically the European Elections and the political context in which they take place. Nor should it be forgotten that the German Basic Law lays especial emphasis upon the German government's role in promoting European integration.

The development of European political parties is a priority for the Union. The linking of the Presidency of the Commission to the European Elections, foreshadowed in the Lisbon Treaty, would also enable European electors to see a direct outcome to the casting of their ballots. In the longer term, simplification of the complicated decision-making of the European Parliament would also lead to greater political transparency. These steps would of themselves do much to help the emergence of a 'demos' for the European Union. In the modern world, it is at least a necessary and often a sufficient condition for belonging to a 'demos' that its members participate in common elections, which lead to decisions affecting the voters and which they regard as legitimate largely because of their participation in these elections. A supranational European Union demands for its full legitimacy supranational democracy. Unless we are to regress to the absurd proposition that the nation state is always and everywhere the fount of all political legitimacy, the European Parliament must always be at the heart of the European Union's political structure.

–o0o–

The existence and activities of the European Court of Justice are a natural consequence of the institutional structure described above. While the European Commission has the task of monitoring the application of European law, agreed by governments and the European Parliament, the European Court of Justice has the final responsibility for interpreting this law in cases of genuine dispute. It is very difficult to see what other institutional arrangements could have been set up for the Union. For the member states themselves to sit as judge and jury on their own interpretation of European law would be plainly indefensible. Those in this country and elsewhere who reject as a matter of principle the underlying institutional structure of the Union will naturally also question the findings of the Court, particularly when directed against the activities of the British government. It is hardly surprising national governments should on occasion resent unwelcome findings by the Court. Nobody enjoys losing a legal action. But it is only in Britain that such resentment normally stems from a fundamental rejection of the political philosophy on which the Court is founded.

–o0o–

The European Union is its institutional framework and the institutional framework is the European Union. Those who claim to support the European Union, but reject its institutions are either personally confused or deliberately misleading their audiences. It is no coincidence that decades of abuse of the European institutions by successive British governments claiming to act as protectors of Britain's position within the European Union have only had the perverse, if predictable, effect of further alienating British public opinion from the Union itself. In more recent times, New Labour's favoured pose as the protector of the British public against the overweening ambitions of the European institutions was in no way reassuring to British public opinion. On the contrary, it encouraged the misperception of the European institutions as entities entirely remote from the United Kingdom, in which British ministers, British officials and British members of parliament played no role.

New Labour apologists in the last decade often argued

that their unenthusiastic approach to the European institutions was necessary to convince the British public that the Union was not on the way to becoming, as the Conservative Party feared and the United Kingdom Independence Party definitely predicted, a European 'federal superstate'. On this analysis, British voters should be persuaded that the British government which they had elected was firmly in the saddle of European decision-making, with the underlying structures of this decision-making predominantly intergovernmental. The European institutions were therefore to be seen as a colourful and self-important distraction from the real work of the European Union, which was to bring national governments together on a co-operative basis, allowing the good sense and political wisdom of national ministers and parliamentarians to establish and develop areas of common activity to the advantage of all. The European Union, claimed Mr. Blair and those who thought like him, should cease to concern itself with institutional questions and start 'delivering' concrete material benefits to its concerned citizenry.

Nobody would deny the importance of economic questions in the European Union's proper functioning. The Union's internal market is one of its most significant achievements and a major contributor to economic growth over the past twenty years. But it is shallow and unrealistic to believe that the single market could have been achieved without the institutional structure of the Union to give it birth and to foster its growth. Without the greater use of majority voting in the Council of Ministers introduced by the Single European Act in 1986 and without the implementation of the Council's decisions by the Commission and the European Court of Justice, the single European market would have remained a purely theoretical aspiration. Recent events in the Eurozone have reminded those who needed to be reminded of the limitations of purely intergovernmental decision-making fora.

Far from needing to choose between the practicalities of economic integration and an abstruse concern with the workings of its institutions, the European Union knows from its history that effective and practical action can result only from strong central institutions. The almost total failure of the much-trumpeted Lisbon (economic) Agenda in the first decade of this century is very much a case in point. Presented by Mr. Blair and Mr. Campbell in the year 2000 as a programme whereby national governments would bypass the traditional institutional fetishes of the Union in order to 'deliver' primarily by intergovernmental co-ordination a markedly improved economic performance in Europe, the Agenda had by 2010 become a laughing-stock. The Agenda's failure to comprehend the vital role of the European institutions in the Union's successes condemned it to ineffectiveness from the beginning.

To the original signatories of the Treaty of Rome, the failure of the Lisbon Agenda would have come as no surprise. They understood two basic truths, which many in the United Kingdom still struggle to understand, even if they regard themselves as being generally favourable to the process of European integration. The first of these truths is that economics and politics cannot be separated. The Treaty of Rome sees European economic integration as serving an explicitly political purpose and political instruments are set up by the Treaty to bring about this economic integration. It is a fantasy to imagine that member states of the European Union can simply participate in the economic aspects of the Union without equal participation in its political structures. The second truth enshrined in the Treaty of Rome is an institutional truth, that a supranational organisation needs supranational institutions. The over-arching ambition of the European Union is to remedy the manifest inadequacies – be these political, economic, environmental or security-related – of the traditional European system of member states. It is inconceivable that this ambition should be realised only by the actions of nation states, without the intervention of supranational institutions.

-oOo-

A recurrent lament of too many in the United Kingdom who certainly would not regard themselves as Eurosceptics is that the European institutions regard themselves, or are regarded by others as being the supposed precursors of a 'federal superstate'. Ironically, the intellectual confusion which the latter concern reflects is probably more damaging to public perceptions of the Union in this country than is unvarnished Euroscepticism.

The fact of the matter is that in joining the European Union, the United Kingdom and other countries made themselves part of a particular political and legal structure in which the European institutions play a leading role. This structure can accurately be described in important respects as 'federal' in character. The supremacy of European law, majority voting in the Council of Ministers, the single currency, the directly-elected European Parliament, the independence of the European Commission, the (small) central budget of the Union and its ability to sign international treaties are undeniably federal components of the Union's structure of governance. The Union would not and could not function without these components to its workings. To view these necessary components of a successful Union with suspicion simply because they can be regarded as 'federal' in their nature is plain bigotry. Many British commentators like to regard themselves as 'pragmatic' in their approach to the European Union. The frequent assumption in this country that patriotic citizens of the United Kingdom must always and in all circumstances be hostile to every evolution of the European Union which could be described as 'federalist' is wholly lacking in anything that can plausibly be regarded as 'pragmatism'.

In some respects, the Union already resembles a traditional state, notably those characteristics listed above as the 'federal' elements of the Union. In other respects, it is very far from being a traditional state, without a substantial central budget, without an army, without a central government, without autonomous tax-raising powers and without bureaucratic structures capable of directly enforcing its decisions. It is extremely unlikely that the European Union will ever precisely resemble in its competences and capacities a member state such as the United Kingdom. It would be surprising indeed if the member states of the Union saw any interest for themselves in the creation of what would now be a twenty-eighth member state to exercise domination over them. On the other hand, the Union is evolving. It is possible, indeed likely, that the Union will acquire more state-like characteristics over the coming years.

In the current bilious and self-centred debate on Britain's role in the European Union, both the principal sides of the argument appear to take a perverse delight in misrepresenting the nature of the Union. It is obvious why the Union's radical critics should have an interest in doing so. It is a historic miscalculation that too many of the Union's self-proclaimed friends in this country believe that acquiescence in at least part of this misrepresentation will add to their credibility with the British public in discussing European questions. All the history of the past twenty years suggests the precise opposite.

Chapter Six:
The press and Europe:
Media McCarthyism

Central to the perversion of thought and rhetoric in the British European debate over the past fifteen years has been the role of the mass media, particularly the populist press. The authors will advance two propositions. First, nothing has contributed more to the current climate of cowardice among even pro-European politicians, or of puzzlement and genuine public unease about the European Union, than the relentless bombardment of anti-European media propaganda, much of it distorted and unbalanced when not actually invented. Second, for different but related reasons, the British media have never in a century been generally less free, impartial, informative and pluralist, or more trivia-obsessed and downmarket – far more so than the media of either continental Europe or North America.

Obviously we are particularly concerned here with the relentless drip-feed of anti-European poison that has seeped into the British political and public consciousness over the past quarter century. But a few initial observations about the value changes that have affected the British press in recent years are worth making. True, the press in Britain has always attracted a strange form of buccaneering, self-promoting tycoons - who, not being content with mere money-making, are anxious for a wider stage. These men seek to influence public opinion and hobnob as superiors to statesmen, as well as socialise with celebrities. Hence the Beaverbrooks, Harmsworths, Pearsons and Hartwells of the past. They were never particularly driven by a political agenda as such, rather inflamed by the passions of their day – Beaverbrook (a friend of Churchill) for example was vigorously anti-appeasement during the 1930s, in contrast to Harmsworth and even The Times (under the editorship of Geoffrey Dawson). Later the Beaverbrook press was vigorously anti-European, out of nostalgia for empire, while much of the press was in favour.

The eccentricity of these tycoons at least guaranteed the plurality of views necessary to a healthy democracy. For them newspapers were largely the toys of wealthy men who had made their fortunes elsewhere, rather than being the sources of those fortunes themselves. In addition there were what might be deemed as philanthropic newspapers, such as the Manchester Guardian, which ironically – because run on a shoestring – were often more commercially administered than those of the moguls.

Starting with Rupert Murdoch's takeover of a large swathe of the press in the 1980s, this began to change. Murdoch's fortune (unlike that of his predecessor as owner of the then influential Times, Lord Thomson) depended on making money from his newspapers. This blurring of the boundaries between tabloid and quality press was unique to Britain: in New York, for example, the New York Post caters to one market, the New York Times to another. The regional newspapers in the US are serious productions, as are the main French newspapers; even tabloids in Italy (La Repubblica) and Spain (El Pais) are high-minded productions. The relentless drive downmarket is uniquely British and entirely commercially driven. It is little exaggeration to say that it has set the cultural standards of a generation, where vulgarity and ignorance are idolised, and intellectual development and serious debate are marginalised or even treated with contempt.

Yet down-market vulgarisation in chase of falling circulations alone does not explain the herd-like stampede of the press into the anti-European corral over the past quarter century. The British public had voted overwhelmingly in the 1975 referendum to stay in Europe and, before the arrival of the tsunami of Europhobic press propaganda, was probably broadly favourable to European integration, albeit with a significant minority always vigorously opposed. There was no reason at that time to believe that an anti-European stance would sell newspapers. Rupert Murdoch and those who thought the way he did are a worrying demonstration of the power of the British press to shift in a generation underlying attitudes.

Unlike, for example, the anti-European Beaverbrook, with his romantic and outdated notions about the British empire, Murdoch loathed the haughty airs of the British imperial establishment and promoted the concept of Britain as a loyal ally of the United States. By contrast,

Black, who was North American (Canadian) by origin, had none of Murdoch's hostility to the British upper classes, but was much influenced by the Eurosceptic Prime Minister, Margaret Thatcher, and his own friends on the American neo-conservative right.

With the two biggest and most influential quality newspaper groups now pursuing a vigorously anti-European agenda; with the Murdoch-owned mass media The Sun and the News of the World, and the Harmsworth tabloid press (the Mail and until recently the Evening Standard) embracing such an agenda because its circulation base was among the normally anti-European conservative right; and with the smaller Express group taking its traditional line, only the Daily Mirror among the red tops provides today a slightly more positive view on European issues (although its fraudster proprietor Robert Maxwell was no Euro-enthusiast), while only the much smaller-circulation Guardian, Financial Times and Independent provide an intelligent counterpoint.

The broadcast media are a little more balanced, although Murdoch's creation of the vastly popular Sky network provides a powerful platform for Europhobic views (some TV anchors and journalists try and resist this, with little success). The BBC and ITV are on the whole neutral on European issues, although both suffer from being over-reactive to the daily agenda of the overwhelmingly anti-European press. They certainly do not provide a counterpoint.

It is hard to overstate the relentlessness with which this anti-European view has been propagated by the overwhelming majority of the British press over the last quarter of a century. The press is not free at all: it is intensely hierarchical when it comes to matters that a proprietor feels strongly about. One senior journalist we know witnessed a major proprietor, immediately after being called in by Mrs Thatcher, whom he strongly supported, as she was being toppled, angrily berating his editor and stomping around the newsroom to ensure that sympathetic articles were written. Any editor, who holds his job entirely on the proprietor's sufferance, will ensure that the latter is never offended by the newspaper's content on such matters.

A British journalist who violates the ethos of his profession and writes a negative story on Europe that happens to be false will receive commendation and promotion (as has happened). By contrast, one with a true story that is positive about Europe is likely to have it 'spiked' (not run) and his career prospects will suffer. In this climate of media McCarthyism, with professional ruin facing a journalist true to his professional ethics, time and again misleading or outrightly false stories about some supposed European excess receive front-page billing.

The creation of the euro in 1999 and the introduction on 1st January 2002, of notes and coins is surely the most obvious case. Time after time most British newspapers assured the British public that there was no possibility of the euro's coming into existence. When it did we were told it would collapse after a few months: more than a decade later we are still waiting. It was asserted by the great majority of the press that the currency would be a pathetic failure: as its value crept up against the pound and the dollar this was dismissed as merely the result of an over-restrictive monetary policy compared with more sensibly flexible US policies (which everyone now recognises were highly irresponsible, simply inflating to fight hugely expensive foreign wars). For two years now the great majority of the British press has asserted that the euro is on the verge of collapse as a result of the Eurozone crisis. Whatever the reason anyone buys British newspapers it surely cannot be that they wish to be well-informed.

Most British politicians, timid over EU matters, are turning their nervousness into a spectator sport called 'keeping foreigners at bay, except the USA'. This has had a corrosive and long-lasting effect on public opinion. Seeing all the double-speak and fear in their political leaders' faces they naturally become euro-hesitant too. This has been especially strong in most recent times as economic austerity and joblessness, deflation and cuts in welfare are increasing anxiety everywhere. The Eurozone crises in 2010 and 2011 were godsends to this process of intellectual and emotional attrition. The universality of this massive daily onslaught on Europe was bound to have an enormous impact on the British public view of the Union.

The UK press, even sometimes decent newspapers too, routinely present the Union as corrupt, undemocratic, overbloated with bureaucracy, overpaid, and arrogant. The individual policy pronouncements of, for instance, the Commission are fitted into this overall excoriation. Apart from the Commission's own discretionary powers under EU law, its policy declarations – in one form or the other – actually usually emanate originally from requests by the member governments meeting in the Council. Conveniently the press fail to mention that fact.

To hammer home the hate campaign, the obsession with so-called sovereignty is now at its hysterical peak in regular pronouncements, even by politicians in the present governing Coalition. Indeed, as we have seen, Section 13 of their agreement between the two parties is actually a defence of this concept to ensure that the Community's power-pooling ethos is kept at bay. Hence this country is now the only member state where leading sections of political opinion, as well as the chauvinistic daily press, campaign for our withdrawal from the Union, some 38 years after we joined. And yet as we have noted above we took over a decade to join!

Britain is now reaching a dangerous stage in our shaky half-hearted membership of the EU. The others are fed up with our repeated and strident intransigence (the UK has more current opt-outs than any other member state---the great majority of member states have none). The future development of the Union is supported by all the others. They want to use the Treaty of Lisbon as the way ahead. If we carry on as we are we run the risk of being asked to leave the Union, to become a dotty, eccentric offshore satrap of an increasingly dysfunctional United States. The European Council of December 2011 has brought this prospect measurably closer.

It would be amusing if it was not so sad, but in fact it was John Major and then Tony Blair in turn who proved more irresponsible than even Thatcher, in allowing this Europhobic hatred to unfold slowly and insidiously. Major and Blair became scared of Rupert Murdoch's and Conrad Black's press and many of their back-bench supporters followed this cowardly example. These island-hopping tycoons were thrilled that their backdoor visits to No.10 Downing Street were paying off in such a tangible way. There was no way the long-suffering British public could receive any alternative to the propaganda onslaught of keeping the European Union at bay as a dangerous wild animal.

It is the phrase 'British interests' that is repeatedly the fatal key to this nonsense. For that is the carry-all excuse for this country refusing again and again to support the key reforms necessary to make the Union function properly. In France, equipped also with a proud, indeed nationalistic tradition, the interests of France and the Union coincide, even with an often strident President Sarkozy. The same applies in Germany, in the sense that 'them' means 'us' as well. In recent years the use of the immortal phrase 'British Interests' has increased. It is now used every day even by Liberal Democrat spokespeople, not as a reassuring coinciding link with similar European interests, but as a device to avoid even treaty obligations.

Mercifully for the remaining good Europeans in this country, as well as in all other member states this British defiance will not work. Since Maastricht, Nice, Copenhagen and now Lisbon, the Union can justifiably request that all member states understand the Union as a legal and geopolitical body in its own right, with its own unified interests. It is not just the sum of its parts in the supposedly 'sovereign' member countries.

However, commonsense does not apply to the continuing farce of the European debate in the British parliament. More of the same pantomime will continue, unless the Coalition begins to find the courage to explain Europe properly to a bemused UK public. From Major's shuffling attempts to deal with the 'bastards' in his own party the centre of gravity shifted under Blair to appeasing the foreign-based press tycoons. The famous myth list expanded apace as the news items from Brussels were bent into shape to fit into UK politicians' prejudices and the new phraseology flourished of 'red lines' against European developments designed to help every member of the Union.

Any selection of press stories from these years onwards would be so vast as to require ten thick volumes. Here we mention just a few of the gems coming from press articles and parties' pamphlets. [1] The Queen was to be stripped of her powers as sovereign. Her face would be taken off the banknotes. There was to be a European army, preferably secret. French police could invade Kent at will. Bananas must be straight and not only yellow. The UK would lose its seat at the UN. Brussels would ban the British pint or Cumberland sausages, and car boot sales and cheese. One of the authors was even attacked for praising the Social Chapter which the 1997 Labour government had accepted, or saying we should sing the EU anthem at all meetings in Britain. The same author, receiving regular hate mail as an MP for being keen on Europe, used to derive great pleasure from replying to such venomous letters with the reminder: 'You know the Royal family are German by origin, as was Queen Victoria's beloved husband'.

There is some strength in the argument that despite these earlier hilarities, the traditional commonsense evident in British politics in previous decades would have seen such attacks diminish and fade away. Far from this being the case, the hostility and distortions have actually increased despite two recent developments which should have encouraged the pro-EU lobby. The first was the Lisbon Treaty itself, which happily brought with it Labour's first full and unequivocal expressions of Euro-enthusiasm both as a party and as a government, thanks partly to the surprisingly new-found courage of even Gordon Brown as Prime Minister. The second was the arrival of the first-ever postwar Coalition administration.

But the same problem reoccurred. The foreign-owned press went into hysterical overdrive to take advantage of the Tories' position as the lead party, reinforced by a major intake of anti-EU young fogies, as well as the usual suspects like William Cash MP. The Daily Mail wrote in November 2010:

> **'Stand firm on EU**
> The most treacherous act of the last parliament was the breaking of the promise, by all three major parties, to hold a referendum on the Lisbon Treaty.
>
> So we welcome the legislation introduced by the Coalition yesterday, stating there can be no further significant transfer of powers from Westminster to Brussels without a public ballot.
>
> If Labour – by far the most guilty party over Lisbon – has a shred of respect for the electorate, it will back this Bill and say that it too will not consent to major EU power grabs without a referendum.'

The implosion of the News of the World in 2011 owing to the squalid phone hacking scandal must offer hope that one dynasty's extraordinary stranglehold over our press, politicians and moral values is slipping, particularly because of American press scrutiny of News International's alleged transgressions. At the very least this Australian-born, US naturalised mogul's simple-minded world view should no longer continue to intimidate or dominate the British political scene in relation to Europe. But there have been many false dawns before: Conrad

Black's downfall and replacement by the Barclay brothers has signified no shift in that newspaper group's tired beating of the anti-European drum. Wholesale reform is long overdue: in particular, a much firmer anti-monopolistic media regime; a right to individual privacy except where publication is clearly in the public interest; similar restrictions on foreign ownership of the British press as exist elsewhere in Europe, and the US.

Never before, on an issue of such compelling national importance as Britain's place in the world, has the press provided such a nearly unanimous chorus of misinformation and shoddy thinking. Never before have elected politicians been so craven in the face of a handful of unelected plutocrats whose antics and viewpoints would be laughable but for the power over public information they wield. Political cowardice, as well as much as press excess, has been responsible for the pursuit of an international destiny so clearly against Britain's own real interests.

Inevitably, too, there will come a moment when it is clear that the emperor has no clothes, just as happened with trade union power in the early 1970s. If anti-Europeanism were really the UK's dominant political philosophy the Conservatives under the (then) Europhobic William Hague, Iain Duncan Smith and Michael Howard ought to have triumphed during the three elections following 1997; on the contrary the Conservatives' obsession with Europe cost them those elections overwhelmingly. As in Alice in Wonderland, the British people, always much more intelligent than either their rulers or the press, will suddenly exclaim, 'you're nothing more than a pack of cards', and the whole bizarre collection of press tycoons, spin doctors, and isolationists and propagandists will fly away.

[1] For a fuller list, see Appendix.

Chapter Seven:
No such thing as society

In May 1988, the then President of the European Commission, Jacques Delors, was invited to speak at the annual gathering of the Trade Union Congress in Brighton. Traditionally, those on the left of the British political spectrum had been divided in their approach to the European Community. Some, like Roy Jenkins and Shirley Williams, were among the most enthusiastic advocates of British membership in the 1970s. Others, including prominent trade unionists such as Hugh Scanlon, were hostile to the process of trade liberalisation implicit within the European treaties, seeing it as an opportunity for rich individuals and companies to enhance their economic dominance at the expense of workers and their living standards.

Mr. Delors hoped to reassure the trade unionists gathered in Brighton that, far from being a 'rich man's club', the European Community would be a vehicle for progressive social policies. He was at least partly successful. His speech in 1988 was certainly one of the factors contributing to a more positive view of the European Community on the left of British politics in general and among trades unionists in particular in the late 1980s and early 1990s. Unfortunately, his speech also provoked on the right of the British political spectrum a simultaneous and very different reaction. What Mr. Delors achieved in the way of reassuring trade unionists was more than outweighed by the concerns he generated on the right and the opportunity he gave for mischief-making by those seeking another route of expression for their anti-European resentments.

In his speech, Mr. Delors made two fundamental errors. He overstated the extent to which European social legislation is capable of changing the differing economic models prevalent in the individual member states of the European Community; and he allowed the trade unionists in his audience to believe that he was offering them, through European legislation, an opportunity to advance by external means their domestic political battle against the Conservative economic policies of the 1980s, which were so uncongenial to the Labour Party and its allies in the trade unions.

Mr. Delors probably thought of himself as simply seeking to combat misconceptions prevalent among his audience, notably that the European Community and the single European market so favoured by the Conservative Party were simply vehicles of remorseless liberalising capitalism. But much of the course of the British debate on Europe over the past twenty years would have been different had he spent more time thinking about the likely reaction of listeners outside the hall.

Prominent among these listeners was Mrs Thatcher, whose animosity towards the European Union and Mr. Delors personally had grown throughout the 1980s. His speech seemed to confirm precisely her worst fears about the likely course of European integration, raising the spectre of an all-powerful executive in Brussels which would reverse the revolution of liberal deregulation upon which she and her Conservative colleagues were engaged in the United Kingdom. Mrs Thatcher was at heart unsympathetic to that project and all the more so if its construction proceeded upon anything other than the rigorously deregulatory lines which she saw as the proper template of public administration. In September 1988, Mrs Thatcher made her celebrated speech to the European College at Bruges, in which she said that 'we have not successfully rolled back the frontiers of the state in Britain, only to see them reimposed at a European level with a European superstate exercising a new dominance from Brussels'. This was a conscious riposte to the speech of Mr. Delors. Its polemical misrepresentations are the mirror images of those employed by the President of the European Commission. The clash of misrepresentations between left and right on social policy has been a defining component of the European debate over the past twenty years, particularly, but not only, in the United Kingdom.

Even twenty years after the speeches of Mr. Delors and Mrs Thatcher it must be clear to any objective observer that the domestic social policies pursued by differing member states of the Union are widely disparate and reflect predominantly national choices in this area. Moreover, these national choices change over time. The reforms in the

German labour market over the past decade have made the economy quite different from what it was in the 1980s. The approach of the current French president, Nicolas Sarkozy, to social questions is a long way removed from that of his predecessor-but-one François Mitterrand or indeed that of Mr. Delors. Since 1997 Britain has been a signatory of the Social Chapter of the Maastricht Treaty, a document which Mr. Major refused to sign at the conclusion of the Treaty in 1991. Yet the workings of British employment and other social legislation are distinct from those of our neighbours, although less so than is sometimes supposed. This similarity is not a consequence of harmonising European legislation, but of the adoption by successive British governments of a social model which is demonstrably European rather than American.

It is not the least of the paradoxes of British politics over the past twenty years that governments have been prepared, even eager, to stress the very few elements of British social policy which resemble the United States rather than the many elements which belong to the European mainstream. American commentators are under no such misapprehension. For them, the economic system of the United Kingdom firmly represents a socialistic European conception of the state, with levels of taxation and social provision which would be inconceivable in the United States. The supposed deficiencies of the British National Health System, for instance, were frequently cited in the recent debate surrounding Mr. Obama's health reforms, almost always as an example of the feared dangers inherent in 'socialised medicine'. While British levels of taxation have in recent years usually been at the lower end of the European spectrum, they and the level of governmental social provision which corresponds to them, are unimaginably higher than even the most radical domestic critic of American laissez-faire capitalism would be prepared to advocate.

Conversely, under the influence of his hosts from the British trade union movement, Mr. Delors seems to have accepted uncritically the thesis that under Mrs Thatcher's government the United Kingdom ceased to be an economy based on European social values and became an economic outpost of the United States, following a purely Anglo-Saxon social model. This misconception was at the root of his often repeated later accusation that the United Kingdom was gaining an unfair competitive advantage within the European Union by its ruthless disregard of social solidarity and the Darwinian conditions of its domestic labour market. Mrs Thatcher and her disciples were only too pleased to adopt this caricature of British social conditions. The caricature may well have corresponded to the social conditions she would have liked to create, or in her more wistful moments she believed she had.

But the past twenty years demonstrate that the United Kingdom, like all its neighbours, is a mixed market economy, in which the state takes upon itself, and is expected to do so by the great majority of its citizens, responsibility for the general well-being of society well beyond that which the United States has traditionally been prepared to envisage. In fairness to Mrs Thatcher, the New Labour government which took office in 1997 was increasingly willing, on ever more slender evidence, to depict the United Kingdom as a fully signed-up member of the Anglo-Saxon economic empire. Its original endorsement of the European Social Chapter in 1997 rapidly gave way to a sour disparagement of supposedly discredited and unsustainable social practices on the other side of the Channel.

New Labour was always an opportunistic scavenger in its rhetoric, not least on European issues. But its willingness to embrace, at least partially, the Thatcherite critique of the European Union in regard to social policy is another interesting example of a phenomenon we have already observed, namely that British perceptions of the European Union are not primarily derived from what it is or does. They are derived primarily from uncertain British ideas about themselves, among which is the hope (it would be too much to describe it as a belief) that they are different to and better than their European neighbours. The debate about European social policy in this country can only be understood in these terms.

The average Briton does not recognise the contribution the European Union has made (modest but real) to raising social standards throughout Europe over the past twenty years. Almost everywhere else, this broad raising of social standards is regarded as a definite success, with the Union's specific contribution to this process often being exaggerated for rhetorical effect by its partisans. Yet, in the United Kingdom European social policy is almost never regarded positively. If British workers today have more rights, if the disabled have more rights, if there is greater economic equality between the sexes, if part-time employees have more rights as a result of European action, none of these improvements figure on the credit side of the ledger of British popular attitudes towards the Union.

Indeed, such improvements are frequently depicted even in the populist press as economic shackles on entrepreneurs, undermining growth and employment, politically correct impediments to the proper functioning of the

British market economy dreamt up by small-minded bureaucrats in Brussels. It is of course perfectly open to analysts or economists to argue that a particular measure of European social action strikes the wrong balance between social protection and economic dynamism. What is striking and specific to the United Kingdom is that when Europe is concerned, it is taken for granted by wide tranches of British public opinion that the wrong balance has been and will always be struck by the Union. In non-European contexts, British public opinion is not convinced that minimal regulation, low taxation on companies, private provision of public services and casualisation of labour are always and everywhere the appropriate social and economic model for their country. When British electors are told however that European action will or may act as a check on the development of this model, many seem to forget their reservations.

The debate about European social policy in this country is not really a debate of political substance. If it were, there is no conceivable reason why the United Kingdom, a country firmly in the mainstream of European social policy in its attitudes and domestic policies, should appear to find the question so contentious. As so often in the European debate in this country, the issue is rather one of identity. Mrs Thatcher had a definite, if unsophisticated sense of national identity. In marked contrast to her male Conservative colleagues who had fought in the Second World War, such as Edward Heath and William Whitelaw, the essential political lesson she drew from events between 1939 and 1945 was that the most natural and appropriate political alignment for the United Kingdom was towards the United States. It had been a mistake of her detested predecessor, Edward Heath, to attempt to reorientate Britain politically towards the European mainland. The member states of the European Union had shown themselves unreliable allies in war and in peace had been altogether too willing to allow themselves to embrace consensual forms of government and political philosophy, such as social and Christian democracy. It is doubtful whether Mrs Thatcher ever clearly differentiated in her own mind between these two latter political philosophies. Certainly she regarded them both with intense suspicion. A more integrated European Union, she feared, would inevitably reflect the political values of solidarity, consensus and broad action by the state in the social field, values which she regarded as by definition socialistic, and wholly incompatible with her personal vision of Conservatism and the British national identity.

Mrs Thatcher saw a pleasing contrast between her caricature image of continental Europe and another she cherished, that of the United States of America, doughty comrade-in-arms of the United Kingdom during the fight against tyranny in the Second World War. It has often been remarked that Mrs Thatcher liked on occasion to give herself Churchillian airs and the apparent continuation of the Grand Alliance 40 years later with the affable President Reagan reinforced this self-image. Nobody who has read the latter volumes of Winston Churchill's war memoirs can fail to observe his resentment at the way in which, as he saw it, America deprived Britain of many of the fruits of its victory in the Second World War, not least in the effective destruction of the British Empire, enthusiastically encouraged by the United States in the 1940s.

But like many in the United Kingdom's political elite, Mrs Thatcher preferred to cling to the reassuring myth of the 'special relationship,' a myth which did after all represent one coherent (if demeaning) view of Britain's position in the world, as the most loyal vassal of the United States of America. The one-sided nature of this relationship, as manifested in the Suez crisis, the invasion of Grenada and even in the early stages of the Falkland Islands war, was not a matter to which Britain's political elite cared to draw attention in public, or perhaps even to recognise in private. The extraordinary apparent belief of one of Mrs Thatcher's successors, David Cameron, that America had been fighting with the United Kingdom against Germany as early as 1940 is a testament to how much Anglo-American relations in recent decades have been sustained by myth-making rather than historical facts.

Indeed Mrs Thatcher brought to the relationship a new element of self-delusion, that Britain and the United States of America shared important similarities in their economic and social systems, and that it was a proper role of British political leaders to emphasise and develop these. Those British leaders who regarded continental Europe as a more natural and attractive point of reference for social and political values were selling the British people short. The rugged individualism of American culture, its deep distrust of the state and its deregulated economy made for a social model much more in harmony with the deepest promptings of the British national identity, one which admittedly had recently been overlain by years of socialism, but which was now triumphantly being restored by the untiring efforts of Mrs Thatcher.

Before Mrs Thatcher, no British Prime Minister of the post-war era would have regarded as remotely plausible her perceptions of British and American social attitudes and alleged similarities between them. Nor was Mrs Thatcher rash enough to pursue policies which led the United Kingdom towards a more American model of society. 'The National Health Service is safe in our hands' was an assurance she knew she had to give in 1983 to maintain the credibility of the Conservative Party as an institution reflecting British public values. How safe is a separate question, but she showed grudging recognition of the popularity of that particular British institution.

True, in the 1980s political choices were made by Mrs Thatcher's government that might not have been made by earlier governments, which at the margin make British arrangements somewhat more like those of the United States. The reduction of tax rates for high earners, the idolisation of financial services and some limited changes in employment law can fairly be cited. But to regard such changes, the first two of which have anyway shown themselves to be unsustainable, as constituting a sea-change in British social attitudes, is preposterous. It is a testament to the dominant role that Mrs Thatcher played in the political discourse of the United Kingdom in the last quarter of the twentieth century that her fanciful ideas should have been taken so seriously, by her supporters, by her opponents and by her later imitators.

When John Major negotiated the final text of the Maastricht Treaty he presented, as a triumphant success for his personal diplomacy, the British opt-out from the Social Chapter. Initially, this mean-minded obeisance to the prejudices of his predecessor was rightly criticised by the opposition, who undertook to reverse it when elected to office. In particular, Mr. Blair and his colleagues scoffed at the alarmist Conservative claim that the introduction of a national minimum wage in the United Kingdom, long a central controversy in European social policy, would destroy thousands of British jobs and blunt British competitiveness. When New Labour took power in 1997, they introduced a national minimum wage. In 2011, that decision was voted one of the most successful British policies of the past thirty years by the leading British academics who make up the prestigious Political Studies Association.

However, New Labour's accession to power in 1997 did not mark the end of the British political elite's difficult relationship with the concept of European social policy. The first decade of New Labour's period in government was a time of relative success for the British economy, fuelled by high oil revenues and the global bubble in financial services. Mr. Blair and, more particularly, Mr. Brown seem rapidly to have convinced themselves that this short-term improvement of British economic performance compared with its European neighbours was the result of exemplary management, producing an economic and social model which others would do well to imitate. Far from needing guidance and inspiration from its European neighbours, the United Kingdom should be regarded as the model of an efficient modernised economy, well-equipped to compete in the globalised market-place. The Conservative Party had perhaps not been entirely wrong in its concern that British competitiveness might be threatened by intrusive and outdated regulatory constraints emanating from Brussels. The representatives of UK-based multinational companies whom New Labour was always eager to court were predictably gratified by New Labour's growing disenchantment with the European Union as a social actor.

The low point of New Labour's posturing to impress British business by its minimalist approach to European social policy was its approach to the European Charter of Fundamental Rights, which the Lisbon Treaty made legally enforceable. In an uncanny echo of John Major's negotiating tactics in 1991, New Labour insisted that it would not be prepared to sign a treaty making the Charter justiciable in the United Kingdom before the European Court of Justice. Ironically, most of the unexceptionable general rights enshrined in the Charter already existed in European legislation, which is legally enforceable in the United Kingdom as elsewhere in the Union. In opting out of the direct legal enforceability of the Charter in the United Kingdom, the British government did little or nothing to combat the threats to economic competitiveness which it claimed to perceive from such dangerous notions as human dignity, freedom of expression, freedom of assembly and the right to engage in collective bargaining (all of which are to be found among the revolutionary contents of the Charter). In the negotiation of the Lisbon Treaty, the British government spent a lot of time and political effort to achieve a non-solution to a non-problem.

For a Labour government to fall over itself to reassure the Confederation of British Industry that in matters of European social policy it had no firmer friend than New Labour was ironic enough. But, even more incoherently, the Conservative Party, when it considered the final text of the Lisbon Treaty, realised that the Treaty had not reversed existing European social and employment legislation, which in some circumstances might be invoked by employees and trade unions against the short-term interests of employers. The Conservative Party does not need long in such circumstances to work out on which side it stands. It entered the General Election of 2010 with a pledge in its manifesto to negotiate a further European opt-out for the United Kingdom, this time from all existing European social and employment-related issues. Mr. Cameron cannot possibly have believed that any such arrangement could be secured with Britain's partners in the European Union. His claim that it could is yet another demonstration of the other-worldly nature of discussion about the European Union in this country, a discussion which often seems to be part of a parallel universe created by the British mass media and their marionettes in Parliament.

In the event, the Conservative Party failed to win an outright majority in the General Election of May 2010. It would be pleasant, if probably over-optimistic, to believe that the Conservative aspiration to strip British voters of all European protection for their social rights contributed to the Party's mediocre result. Few British voters are aware of the real implications for themselves of Conservative hostility to any European social role. Since the General Election, Mr. Cameron has been noticeably more circumspect about his Party's commitment to 'repatriate' social powers to the United Kingdom. The Coalition with the Liberal Democrats has provided a convenient excuse for him to postpone indefinitely an aspiration which is unrealisable and would be deeply unpopular if openly discussed. The British electorate emphatically do not believe that British employers have a uniquely privileged insight into economic rationality and social well-being.

If the Labour Party, freed of the obsession with tactics on European issues of its most recent leaders, were able to engage with the British electorate in a more rational discussion of European social policy, it might well be pleasantly surprised by the political advantage it could derive, both for itself and for public perceptions of the European Union. The auguries however are not good. When in government New Labour proclaimed itself every bit as concerned as its Conservative predecessor about the supposed dangers for patient care of the European Working Time Directive, which limits the hours doctors can work without rest. A political party which is so unwilling to combat anti-European prejudice that it will not explain to the British public the dangers for patient care arising from tired doctors is not a party well-placed to institute a coherent and objective discussion on as controversial a matter as European social policy. The relentless depiction to the British electorate of the defence of their hard-won social rights by the European Union as an unwanted intrusion rather than a welcome reinforcement has, sadly, cut deep in this country over recent decades.

-o0o-

In our often gothically depressing analysis of the deep and continuing anti-Europeanism served up by some unreconstructed (mostly Tory) MPs and the dodgier bits of the mostly overseas-owned UK press, we can sometimes glimpse slightly lighter shades of darkness. The range is one from nervous hesitations – which often reflect respectable anxieties on individual policies – to apathy, fear and pure rage as in The Sun, the Daily Mail and the Express, a rage which is existential in nature. One aspect of the European Union where a relatively mild judgement can be expected from these newspapers is the single market concept, and its principal original apparatus, the Single European Act. For this is concerned with free trade, free business and free markets. In this context integration is not only in order, it is crucial. 'Why are they taking so long to complete the single market?' the anti-Europeans ask. Companies can integrate across national borders as much as and whenever they wish. But this integration must be limited in the Europhobe analysis to companies and similar economic actors. International business spokesmen have often fretted at the signs of trade unions in different member states seeking to internationalise their efforts, through the European Trade Union network, or directly. In any other context than the European one, British public and political opinion would be likely to welcome international co-operation to defend workers' rights and promote good practices at the workplace. That so much of British opinion has been taken in by the anti-social rhetoric of the Eurosceptics when discussing European policy is a striking instance of the way in which anti-European prejudice can all too frequently trump intellectual, political or moral consistency.

Chapter Eight:
The European budget and the
Common Agricultural Policy

In this book we have chronicled the relentless flood of British calumny against the construction of a united Europe. Attacks on the European Parliament as an illegitimate institution, on the Commission as an impertinent usurper, on the Court of Justice as a threat to national law making, all have been the hallmarks of a saga of hatred, never more vitriolic than in the present day Conservative Party.

Nowhere has the rage at all things European been more evident than in the Europhobic lobbies' assault on the EU Budget and on the Common Agricultural Policy. This twin-pronged assault embraces politicians, a proportion of the propaganda sheets that masquerade as newspapers in this country, a bevy of odd-looking think tanks, even the Institute of Directors and the CBI from time to time. What is it about this rather modest piece of financial policy accumulation in the European budget that incites such hysteria and apoplexy? What is it about the Common Agricultural Policy which prevents even normally rational British commentators from sparing a good word for it?

Some of the resentment clearly comes from the often painful history of our gradual, long-drawn-out realisation in the sixties that the UK needed the then EEC more than the other way around. There was no way that the six founding members would allow us to clamber on board fifteen years late and change such fundamentals of the EU Budget as the Common Agricultural Policy. So we were obliged to accept from day one of membership a financial support system of limited net benefit to our own modest farm sector, itself providing less than half our foodstuff requirements. Our attempts to create in the European Regional Fund a counterpoint to the Common Agricultural Policy provoked in the early years of British membership intense suspicion from the German government, which was already the largest contributor to the existing EEC budget.

Since huge party divisions then, as now, bedevilled constructive internal British politics even in the field of international treaties, the ensuing Labour government from 1974 added to the general apprehensiveness over the Brussels budget manoeuvrings in Britain. Major changes in the CAP and other items were demanded by that Labour government as well as 'fairer methods of financing the Community budget'. As the existing member states, although dismayed and puzzled by such early British intransigence, indicated a willingness to accommodate us, the first steps to appease the least enthusiastic member of the club were taken then. Led by the German Chancellor,

Helmut Schmidt, our partners accepted that our budget share might rise too high by 1980 without some corrective mechanism and were willing to allow Commonwealth meat and dairy producers generous market access terms without Britain's having to offer anything back to the Community. Even so the long-term myth of something being fundamentally wrong with the EEC budget system began at this period to take root in Britain.

Labour's long years of intransigence over EC questions prevented us from having a united front to present to international partners. Mrs Thatcher's even fiercer attitudes to the budget on taking office were shown over the rebate settlement. Once again a generous outcome agreed by our partners was received with less than a smile by the Iron Lady. This outraged the continental negotiators, who recently had witnessed a singular lack of British gratitude for EEC support in the Falklands war, a stance not easy for the Italians, in particular. We forget now that even at this stage some of our partners, led later by the French President, François Mitterrand, began to suggest that the UK should cease to be a full member and settle for residing in a halfway house between full membership and exclusion.

The benefits as a whole of British membership of the European Union can scarcely be compared to a budgetary mechanism that is minuscule at EUR 125 billion, a trivial sum in comparison with many times that figure in the various national budgets of 27 nations. That is the astonishing reality for a policy that has produced considerable benefits to the weaker parts of member states' economies for very little outlay. The British anti-Europeans are resolutely determined, come what may, to ignore the all positive aspects of the EU Budget. For example, and contrary to the usual myths, the control system is strict and improving after years of experience in putting together the wide cultural national differences in budget control procedures of the various member states. The Commission's internal supervision procedures are supplemented by the EU Court of Auditors in Luxembourg, which maintains a very strict control system. Contrary to the hysterical claims of the Europe-haters, the Court has regularly confirmed that the annual budget accounts are correctly drawn up, and give a fair representation of the figures. This is in stark contrast to the mostly British auditors who resolutely certificated the accounts of questionable British banks and fund managers on the eve of one of the biggest financial collapses in history in 2008.

When the Court has reserved its endorsement of accounts, it has usually been because of technical and administrative accounting errors carried out by the member countries' own financial supervisors, on whom they have to rely for an accurate inspection of the money flows invoiced to recipients of the various Budget appropriations. Some 80% of EU spending is now under shared management with the member states, which itself in general reinforces the overall surveillance that sums are spent correctly. The actual incidence of fraud is tiny too. The Court reported only some four cases to the EU anti-fraud office, called OLAF, last year, an entirely marginal figure in comparison with the millions of transactions within the Budget expenditures.

These outturns are much better than those of any single member state. The dreadful overcharging on defence contracts in the UK Ministry of Defence exposes that the real problems lie in national budgets, not communitarian ones. The recent eccentric campaign by UKIP and others to highlight the supposed scandal that the EU costs Britain £45 million a day has rebounded as the public realise that even this doubtful figure is tiny in comparison with what we spend – or waste – on massive defence spending when there is no longer a conventional enemy to guard against, or failing to bring to book tax evaders owing some £150 billion to our Exchequer.

The Europhobes have to concede, if they are fair, that Britain's net contribution to the European Budget remains largely unchanged precisely because of our different patterns of trade with the rest of the world, a different VAT base, excessive imports and a lower farming base. It was never intended that the rebate would last forever, and other member states now claim their (smaller) rebates as well. The Europhobes would be better employed in joining in the urgent task of making sure that the modern Budget system for 2013-20 is fit for purpose in a changing world. The European Budget has in fact usually underspent in recent years, not least because of stricter controls than previously.

Unlike the member states with their vast budget deficits and long-term national debt, the EU Budget is the most virtuous of all in that its receipts equal its payments. It does not raise debt. Moreover the agony of annual budgetary fixing has now been replaced by the financial perspective system which sets binding limits to overall spending and different classes of spending over several years. Finally, the modern EU Budget concentrates only on the small segment of joint policies where collective spending is more rational than spending by a single country. Intercountry research programmes are only one recent example where the EU budget can make a significant contribution.

The Budget allocations of the Union break down into six basic areas; sustainable growth in terms of the Lisbon mark 2 and 3 programmes; natural resources and farming; freedom, security and justice; foreign policies; spending on the institutions; and temporary help to any new nations joining. If only the anti-Europeans would abandon their apoplexy about a very modest budget system bringing the members closer together, they could study it more as a complex but sensible machine for effective financial cohesion. But even complex mechanisms need to adapt to new circumstances. Should the elements in each country's contribution base be examined anew with an open mind?

These revenues come from four sources: customs duties including farm imports; sugar levies on production; the VAT-based payments on the notional 1% rate, and Gross National Income–based contributions, used as the balancing item to prevent the need to borrow. Own resources, the first three of these segments, are now down to a very modest proportion of income, with over three quarters coming from segment four. This reality suggests a possible new source of exclusively owned revenues for the Commission's Budget incomings, such as the proposed financial transactions tax, an idea guaranteed to cause the maximum rage amongst the anti-EU troglodytes in Britain. But why should a tax raised by one nation state be sacred whereas a tiny communitarian tax is sinful?

On the spending side of this complicated international system we note the growing need to consider whether budget modernisation implies adapted, modified, indeed even new uses for the funds. We note that the Federal

Trust a few years ago asserted that 'there are policy areas such as foreign and defence, environment, industrial research, transport and cross-border infrastructure, where the EU component ... is widely accepted by national electorates'. A simultaneous reduction in farm spending to 30% or even 20% of a gradually enlarging budget, concentrating perhaps on the post-2004 member states (except presumably Malta and Cyprus) would provide ample leeway for new purposes and targets for sensible support. The current review of the European Union's budget between 2013 and 2020 provides an opportunity for fresh thinking about both the income-raising and spending sides of the budgetary process. It would be a pity if this opportunity were lost through prejudice, misinformation and sheer bloody-mindedness.

Within the European budget, one sector of EU policy creation and actual support, namely the Common Agricultural Policy, evokes a strange, often equivocal, response from the Europhobes in the United Kingdom. This is not primarily to do with the looming Common Agricultural Policy reform programme, starting after 2013, which enjoys an impressive near unanimity of support amongst most informed commentators. Many different arguments arise over details of the future policy mix, but basically every observer appears to favour fundamental changes and the continuing reduction in cash and market-fixing support for actual production levels. This attitude is less prevalent in the newest member states which often feel that they are losing out to the established larger member states, including Britain. There are often, too, subtle variations in opinion within and between France and Germany, Italy and Spain. An unexpected factor which complicates the response to the European Union's Common Agricultural Policy amongst the British anti-EU tribe is the political and economic tension that arises from age-old structures relating to land – and hence, farm – ownership in the UK.

For many British land-owners, the dilemma posed by the Common Agricultural Policy has always been painful and is becoming more so. For the previous support system with direct subsidies for production and guaranteed markets has – especially with large-scale farmers –produced enormous financial rewards to some in the United Kingdom, benefiting both tenants and owners as well as co-operatives and even food-producing and distribution concerns. Some of the figures of annual subsidy in the United Kingdom have been so large that at least some British land-owners with a sense of decorum refrained from grumbling about the EU too stridently. Many of these land-owners were Tory supporters, although out-and-out rejectionists like UKIP of course maintained their rhetorical attacks on the CAP and called for repatriation of national subventions, which would have been even more expensive. Some very famous British landowners have received huge amounts. To spare their blushes we will not enumerate them here; but a host of accurate websites are available to the curious. A number of old landowning dynasties have received substantial sums from the CAP even if some of their individual clan members loathe the EC and all its devilish works. A final awkward element has augmented British embarrassment. The profile of UK landowning and the preservation of huge private landowner estates – indeed even in the centre of London – has inevitably meant that successive British governments and ministers of agriculture have been reluctant to yield to the Commission's repeated attempts to place a maximum ceiling on total payments to one single legal person, or one individual company or entity.

France has traditionally been the largest total recipient of CAP financial subsidies, but with much smaller average individual payments going to often tiny rural farms. Even these small farmers are now down to little more than 3% of the population directly employed on the land, with more and more working on a contract basis, as in Britain and elsewhere. Britain has received a much smaller total of payments from the CAP, but the maximum payments recorded in this country have far exceeded their French equivalents in all but a few cases, cases that were usually 'collective' farming entities. As major reforms in the CAP seem likely, will these reforms focus on giving proportionate assistance to the weaker, smaller, more vulnerable end of the business, in parallel with payments for modernising, improving and detoxifying the environment?

For the CAP has already shifted away from a traditional price and market support policy, a policy which has actually been much less expensive for the member states than both the US and the Japanese subsidy networks. It is now unfolding as a system of direct payments to sustain farm revenues and foster rural rejuvenation. The 2013-2020 regime is expected to complete the virtual decoupling of direct support, save possibly in a few segments. The underlying aim of the new perspective would be for the Commission to seek the staged but eventual convergence of current payments per hectare, to all receiving farmers in all member states, a system which is supported by the NFU in Britain. This would be the only way to avoid the real social dislocation and political tension that exists if manifestly unfairly differential payments are made in different countries. These repugnant variations are still enormous and they offend the sense of a just and true single market in farm products.

Meanwhile, the old allocations of CAP spending to different countries are no longer justified. This is where the tradition of redistribution housed in European treaty-making must make itself felt. This will only be achievable if the founding members, and the UK, Denmark and Ireland from 1973, show wisdom and geopolitical generosity. After all in the British case, it is not the fault of our partners that our import, trading and farm production patterns are strikingly at odds with theirs for historical reasons. Surely too, part of the farm budget should include funding for R&D in instances where farmers themselves and technical agro-companies may be unable to fill the gap.

In the final analysis, an equitable and balanced new framework for the Common Agricultural Policy is essential, not least to help dampen down the dangerously growing Europhobia in Britain. We may also hope that young, new, technically ambitious farmers, male and female, will not be put off trying to enter into such a potentially inspiring environmental industry. Britain would be much better placed to make a success of contributing to necessary reforms of the Common Agricultural Policy if its political class were able to adopt a more balanced view of the Policy and its workings; and confront the problems for British agriculture arising from the eccentric structure of British land-owning practice, rather than blame the European Union for any conceivable problems in the British agricultural sector.

Chapter Nine: Power to the people?

In November 2009, the leader of the Conservative Party, David Cameron, found himself confronted with a delicate political decision. After months of foot-dragging, the Eurosceptic President of the Czech Republic, Vaclav Klaus, had finally signed his country's instrument of ratification for the Lisbon Treaty. Since the Czech Republic was the last ratifying country for the Treaty, it would thus enter into force on 1st December 2009. Given the vigour with which Mr. Cameron and his party had denounced the Lisbon Treaty, there was considerable political pressure upon him to comment publicly upon this new development and in particular to indicate what steps a Conservative government might take if elected in the forthcoming British General Election. Many Conservatives wanted him to undertake to suspend the application of the Treaty in the United Kingdom until a referendum had been held.

Although Mr. Cameron's instincts are profoundly Eurosceptic in character, he is a much more careful and calculating politician than many in his party, particularly where European issues are concerned. He knows, as some at least of his colleagues do not, that the British electorate is only intermittently interested in European questions and is easily bored by them. Indeed, the party's obsessive concern with European issues was one of the reasons why, for so many years after the Labour landslide of 1997, it was unable to mount any serious electoral challenge to the increasingly unpopular Labour government. To go into the General Election of 2010 with a Conservative manifesto promising a referendum leading to the suspension and likely later abandonment by the United Kingdom of the ratified Lisbon Treaty would be to hand a distinct electoral advantage to the Labour Party. Mr. Brown and his colleagues could argue that the Conservative Party under Mr. Cameron remained the same bitter and backward-looking political formation which its obsession with Europe in particular had long shown it to be. Mr. Cameron did not want to enter the General Election campaign of 2010 having made any such electoral present to his opponents.

Mr. Cameron therefore announced in early November 2009 that the Conservative Party would not seek in office to reopen the question of the ratification of the Lisbon Treaty. While rational, this decision was deeply unwelcome to many in his party. As consolation for the wounded feelings of his more radical Eurosceptic colleagues, he undertook to introduce when in government four new measures to reduce the Treaty's impact and to bind as far as possible the hands of future British governments in their negotiations on possible changes to the European treaties. This compromise, whereby the Conservative Party grudgingly accepted the reality of the Lisbon Treaty, but would work in government to minimise its scope and prevent new treaties in future, saw the party through the General Election, in which European issues figured only marginally.

After the election one of Mr. Cameron's proposed supplementary European measures, to negotiate for the 'repatriation' to the United Kingdom of powers over labour law and social issues, did not even survive the negotiation of the Coalition agreement with the Liberal Democrats in May 2010. That so unrealisable an aspiration should have survived even that long is a testament to the estrangement from international political reality which pervades much European discussion in this country, not least in the Conservative Party. Another of his measures, that the House of Commons could scrutinise in detail any proposed use of the 'bridging clauses' contained in the Treaty of Lisbon for uncontroversial future changes to the existing treaties is of theoretical importance only. The bridging clauses (passerelles) of the Lisbon Treaty allow future minor changes to the Lisbon Treaty to be adopted by a unanimous vote of national governments, without a formal calling of an intergovernmental conference. Mr. Cameron has made it clear that his government will not vote for changes through these 'bridging clauses' and their implementation needs unanimity among European governments. It can even be argued that greater Parliamentary debate on changes brought about by the 'bridging clauses' would be no bad thing as so much nonsense is talked in the Eurosceptic press about the iniquity of these clauses.

The case is very different, however, for the two final measures proposed by Mr. Cameron, which taken together dominated much of the domestic European debate in the United Kingdom in the first half of 2011. The Conservative/Liberal Democrat Coalition's European Union Act is the direct result of these two proposals, the first to make British ratification of any future European treaties dependent upon a referendum; and the second, the controversial Clause 18, to clarify the supposedly pre-eminent role of British Parliamentary sovereignty within the European legislative process. The first of these measures has a certain political logic to it, dangerous and dishonest though it may be; the second lays bare for all to see the intellectual and moral bankruptcy of Euroscepticism as a philosophy of government. It is revealing of the state of opinion within the Conservative Party towards the European Union that Mr. Cameron should have thought it necessary to weld a rational decision to acquiesce in the ratification of the Lisbon Treaty with two such unedifying measures that ought to bring shame upon his government and his party.

-o0o-

Given the obviously partisan and populist nature of the call in the European Union Act for a referendum on any future treaty changes, it may seem politically naive to comment in any detail on the relevant provisions of the Bill. Their goal is simply to make it more difficult for future governments to participate in changes to the European treaties. Some radical Eurosceptic critics have argued that the Bill is defective because it allows changes to the treaties deemed by the government to be 'trivial' to be ratified by the United Kingdom without a referendum. This is no more than a debate at the margins about the precise weight of the shackles to be loaded on future British governments. In a referendum, ignorance about the European Union, fanned ruthlessly by influential newspapers, and topical political issues of the day unrelated to the Union are likely to be decisive in the outcome. It is many years since this country had a government willing to confront populist and elite prejudices in this country about the European Union and Britain's place in it. Such a long-term process of information and education would be a precondition for winning any European referendum in this country. That prospect, for the foreseeable future, is extremely remote.

The approach of the EU Act to referendums is based explicitly in its text upon the proposition that deeper British participation in the European Union is a process whereby British power and sovereignty is 'transferred' away from the United Kingdom and 'surrendered' to the European Union. Any of the traditional notions of 'sharing' British sovereignty, of allowing Britain to participate in a 'wider' sovereignty, or of 'reinforcing' British sovereignty through international action are entirely alien to the Bill's philosophy and rhetoric. European treaties have on this analysis one typical effect and one only: they deprive the British people of 'their' sovereignty and give it to 'others'. Since the central political and institutional rationale of the European Union lies precisely in the pooling of national sovereignties to ensure their more effective, peaceful and rational exercise, it is difficult to see how the reductionist rhetoric of the EU Act is intellectually compatible with Britain's present membership of the European Union, let alone its participation in future European progress.

Mr. Cameron denies, and Mr. Clegg would no doubt be horrified by, the accusation that the Coalition's European policy is a stepping-stone to British withdrawal from the European Union. The underlying assumptions of the European Union Act however point clearly in this direction. They explicitly contradict the only political analysis, that of mutual and enlightened self-interest, on the basis of which the United Kingdom first joined the European Union and whereby British membership of the Union continues to make sense. To that extent the Act marks an important staging-post in a baleful process of self-willed British estrangement from the European Union.

It must be recognised that the Act is part of a process and not an event on its own. Some Liberal Democrats in particular are inclined to present the document as an embarrassing necessity which can soon be forgotten about and in any case is unlikely to have any tangible effects over the lifetime of the Coalition. This is to underestimate the seriousness and determination of the leading Europhobes in this country, both inside and outside the Conservative Party. The latter, as leader of the Coalition government, has anyway made it clear that it will not accept any changes in the European treaties that might trigger a referendum. The EU Act is not directed towards the actions of the present government. It is directed towards its successors, which might be inclined to pursue a less distrustful policy towards our closest allies in the European Union.

It is particularly ironic that the Conservative Party has usually shown no enthusiasm for the exercise of popular sovereignty through referendums. Illuminatingly, the EU Act excludes from the requirement for a referendum any future European treaties relating to the enlargement of the European Union – a sharing of national sovereignty upon which the British government might be expected to have a favourable view, a view not necessarily shared by most British voters. This general Conservative distrust of popular consultations is well illustrated by its attitude to electoral reform. This year's referendum on the subject was a concession wrung unwillingly from the Conservative Party as a price of Liberal Democrat participation in the Coalition: a number of Conservative backbenchers sought to postpone or even prevent its taking place.

Even more significantly, the Conservative Party overwhelmingly favours the system of relative majorities (known misleadingly as 'First Past the Post') for elections to the House of Commons. This system can ensure for an incoming government a handsome Parliamentary majority with 40% of the votes cast, a system which is the apotheosis of representative rather than popular democracy. The current electoral system is often justified by its advocates as an effective way of guaranteeing strong government. There is however one limit for some of these advocates on the strength they wish to see British governments exercising. That limit relates, unsurprisingly, exclusively to European policy. A referendum on a future European treaty can be used as a barricade against any future government wishing to retrieve Britain's position at the centre of European affairs after years of neglect and hostility. Long after this present Coalition government is mouldering in its political grave, it aspires to exercise a restrictive influence on all future British governments in their European policy. Both in its general rhetoric and in its specific provisions, the EU Bill has a good chance of doing precisely that.

This aspiration to bind the actions of future British governments is all the more bizarre in that it comes from a political party supposedly committed to Parliamentary sovereignty. The thesis that no one Parliament can bind its successor is at the very heart of the in many other respects cloudy doctrine of Parliamentary sovereignty. Even stranger, the EU Act accords a specific right to seek judicial review against the decision of any future British government not to hold a referendum about a European treaty change. This provision was inserted to reassure Mr. Cameron's most vociferous backbenchers that the government was doing everything it could to entrench Britain's current semi-detachment from the European Union. The possibility of judicial review has not altogether reassured these backbenchers, but its insertion in the Act is a vivid illustration of the real motivations underlying its detailed provisions.

It will certainly be more difficult as a result of the EU Act for any future government to adopt without a referendum any such future European text as that of the Lisbon Treaty. From the point of view of the Conservative Party, a desirable goal has thus been achieved. No such claim for political coherence can be made for the notorious Clause 18 of the EU Act, which seeks to enshrine in statute the common law doctrine of Parliamentary sovereignty, but which actually casts doubt on the real commitment of the Conservative Party to the doctrine of Parliamentary sovereignty.

Mr. Cameron's speech of November 2009, committing him to introduce legislation on British Parliamentary sovereignty in the European context was particularly carefully phrased, perhaps reflecting a subconscious awareness of the difficulties involved. The concept of British parliamentary sovereignty is a notoriously difficult and controversial one, and its application in the European context is especially problematic.

Parliament voted to take Britain into the European Union in 1972 and could vote to take Britain out at any time. But beyond those two extreme cases, it is far from clear what relevance the slogan of 'British parliamentary sovereignty' can have in the European context. Once a European Directive or Regulation has been properly adopted, the British and other Parliaments are obliged by the treaties they have themselves ratified to give effect to these legal provisions. As long as Britain remains a member of the European Union, certain traditional conceptions of British parliamentary sovereignty remain at best in abeyance. The unsatisfactory text of Clause 18 and the controversy it has provoked should not have been surprising to anyone familiar with this legal and political background.

Many of those pressing Mr. Cameron to introduce Parliamentary legislation on the role of the British Parliament in the European legislative process harboured the hope that this would act as a second brake upon Britain's continuing participation in the development of the European Union. For them, the ideal outcome would have been a text which gave the House of Commons a veto upon every individual piece of European legislation adopted by the Council of Ministers. This outcome would have represented a serious threat to the United Kingdom's continued membership of the European Union, an outcome welcome to many in the Conservative Party. Among Conservative MPs, there is a substantial body of opinion privately, or even publicly, hostile to the very principle of British membership of the Union. Another important body of Conservative Parliamentary opinion would make continued British membership dependent upon changes in Britain's legal obligations within the Union which are politically and legally unachievable.

The latter position was very close to that adopted by the Conservative Party in its manifesto for the 2010 General Election. From that manifesto, it was clear that a failure in government to renegotiate the terms of British membership of the Union in regard to European social and employment law would place in jeopardy the Conservative commitment to continued membership of the Union. Since the General Election Mr. Cameron and his Foreign Secretary, William Hague, have preferred to stress the formal position of the Coalition government, that Britain will continue to be a member of the Union, without this membership being dependent upon renegotiation of its terms, including social and employment law. This understanding of Conservative European policy clearly precluded any legislation on British Parliamentary sovereignty which genuinely changed the existing legal position.

The Coalition and its legal advisers therefore had to resort to abstruse legal argument about the nature of the legislation presented for adoption by Parliament. According to David Lidington, the Minister for European Affairs, speaking to the House of Commons in November 2010:

> The Common Law is clear that the doctrine of Parliamentary sovereignty has not been affected by Britain's membership of the EU ... So we believe there is great merit in putting the matter beyond speculation by affirming the Common Law position in statute, which will reinforce the rebuttal of contrary arguments in the future.

For most parliamentarians, this is simple legal hair-splitting, which the government itself admits will make no difference to the day-to-day operation of British membership of the European Union. The radical Eurosceptics so numerous on the Conservative backbenches had certainly expected something more politically robust from their leaders.

Even the convolutions involved in Mr. Lidington's presentation are legally and constitutionally dubious. Can the anyway fuzzy concept of Parliamentary sovereignty be enshrined effectively in statute by the House of Commons? Arguably, the House would only be entitled to adopt such a statute if it already certainly possessed the claimed sovereignty, a circumstance which would render otiose the whole procedure. It is moreover wholly unclear whether a future House of Commons could, if it wished to, repeal Clause 18, and if it did, what effect, if any, this repeal would have. A similar puzzle arises from any sustained application of the doctrine of Parliamentary sovereignty to the provisions of the EU Bill for referendums on European treaties. There is a perfectly respectable constitutional argument for believing that a future House of Commons would be entitled simply to ignore the provisions of the Bill requiring a referendum on a particular treaty and ratify that treaty as an exercise of the Common Law doctrine of Parliamentary sovereignty. Such is the legal tangle which the Coalition has got itself into.

A sharp distinction therefore needs to be drawn between the two central components of the Coalition's EU Act, that relating to Parliamentary sovereignty and that relating to future referendums. The former is simply a probably unsuccessful effort on Mr. Cameron's part to reassure his backbenchers that he shares their pain at the sovereignty-sharing aspects of the European Union. Sovereignty-sharing is intrinsic to the European Union, but Mr. Cameron was not at the time of presenting the EU Bill, willing to draw one of the two logical conclusions from his party's hatred of the European Union, either to confront and defeat that hatred in all its bitterness and irrationality, or to assuage it by taking Britain out of the European Union.

As long as the Conservative Party's leadership is unable or unwilling to adopt either of these clear options, such absurdities as the debate about the sovereignty of the British Parliament within the European Union are the inevitable consequence. Some will regard this debate as a harmless and an acceptable price to pay for Britain's continued membership of the European Union, to which the Conservative Party remains formally committed. Others will be more concerned that debate on British Parliamentary sovereignty within the European Union is an ugly symptom of the irrationality and self-absorption which usually passes for discussion of European issues in this country. To these observers, the long-term dangers for Britain's position in the European Union of Mr. Cameron's temporising with the forces of unreason and resentment will be more apparent than any short-term benefits.

Introducing the Bill in the House of Commons, Mr. Hague put the other parties on notice that in every future General Election the Conservative Party would be challenging its opponents to say whether they intended to repeal the EU Bill's provisions on referendums. It is sadly difficult to believe that any of today's political parties will have the self-confidence to announce such a step in the midst of a febrile campaign. By the back door, the

Coalition government is seeking to introduce an entrenched commitment to referendums on Europe into the British constitution, an innovation which the Conservative Party would certainly reject with horror in any other context than that of European policy.

A final reflection is perhaps appropriate about the acquiescent role of the junior partner of the Coalition, the Liberal Democrats, in the passage of the EU Act. It is noteworthy that in the House of Commons, Liberal Democrat MPs loyally voted for the Bill, a unanimity not reflected in the House of Lords, but which says much about the centre of gravity on European issues among Liberal Democrat Members of Parliament. Those of them who might otherwise feel embarrassed to be supporting legislation so exclusively animated by the Conservative Party's detestation of the European Union sometimes argued in their defence that the Bill's provisions on Parliamentary sovereignty were simply meaningless. It was moreover unlikely that there would be a new European treaty in the foreseeable future where the holding of a referendum under the new legislation would be a genuine prospect. But there is usually a political price to be paid for unheroic silence in the face of dangerous nonsense. Nick Clegg and the Liberal Democrats have been called upon to pay it in the wake of the disastrous European Council of December 2011. A treaty to reform the governance of the Eurozone is an imminent reality. Britain's attempt to veto its adoption as an amendment to the European treaties marks a disturbing further step towards the United Kingdom's leaving the European Union entirely. Silence and wishful thinking have done much in the past decade to ease the path of Euroscepticism towards political hegemony in this country. The willingness of the Liberal Democrats to support as a price for coalition the EU Bill was an undignified continuation of this depressing tradition. The silence of the remaining pro-European lambs remains deafening.

Chapter Ten:

The Euro through the looking glass

In the months leading up to the General Election of 2010, the three largest political parties resolutely ignored the subject of the single European currency, despite the unprecedented decline in the external value of the pound against the euro during that period and the wholesale destruction of the economic analysis on which British standoffishness towards the euro supposedly rested.

During the election campaign itself, the parties were divided only in the degree of their coolness towards the single European currency. The Conservative manifesto contained a commitment that no Conservative government would ever take Britain into the euro, the Labour manifesto made no reference to the topic at all and the Liberal Democrats paid at best lip service to the remote possibility of joining the euro in the very distant future.

This convergence of views has if anything solidified since the General Election. In the Coalition agreement the Liberal Democrats accepted that the United Kingdom would not join or make any preparations to join the euro over the next five years.

This unusual unanimity between the main political parties might seem the considered, measured and rational view of the British body politic on the question of the euro. In fact, it is rather a proof of the dysfunctional British political system where European questions are concerned. It was convenient indeed for opponents of British membership of the euro that the sovereign debt crisis began in early 2010. It has allowed them to replace one myth, that of the superiority of British economic management to that of the Eurozone, with another about the imminent demise of the European single currency. In due course, the speciousness of this new rationalisation of British economic insularity will no doubt be revealed. The euro is not going to disappear and is likely to emerge from the present crisis reinforced rather than weakened. Almost certainly this very reinforcement will be solemnly presented by those hostile to British membership of the euro as yet another reason why the United Kingdom should never join the European single currency.

Dysfunctionalism has of course been a component of British political life over the past fifteen years, not limited to European questions. The two leading figures of the government during that period, Mr. Blair and Mr. Brown, were locked in a resentful and self-destructive personal and political relationship that paralysed most of New Labour's political decision-making. The thirteen years that New Labour was in office almost exactly coincided with the creation and first decade of the single European currency. New Labour therefore played a central role in defining British public and political attitudes to the euro. European policy was one theatre of war between Mr. Blair and Mr. Brown. It was the public policy of New Labour to keep open the theoretical possibility of British membership of the euro in vaguely-defined appropriate circumstances. New Labour's actions in government however postponed this membership into at least the medium term and perhaps even the long-term future.

Before the General Election of 1997, there were a number of commentators who believed that Mr. Brown was at least as favourable to the idea of British membership of the euro as was Mr. Blair, a position which had radically changed by the autumn of 1997, when the celebrated five 'tests' for British accession to the European single currency were promulgated by Mr. Brown and his advisers. In the following decade Mr. Brown provided an apparent rationale for British non-participation in the euro, one disproved by events, but by no means without influence even today in British perceptions of the European single currency.

As chancellor, Mr. Brown missed few opportunities to underpin his barely concealed hostility towards the euro by underlining the supposed distinctiveness of the United Kingdom and its superiority to the outdated and unreformed economies of its neighbours in Western Europe. Unlike France and Germany, the United Kingdom had understood the need in the modern world for radical economic and particularly financial liberalisation, which found its expression in high levels of personal and corporate debt in the United Kingdom, an ever-growing financial sector and an ever-rising property market which was indispensable to sustain British economic activity in general and personal consumption in particular. The success of the British model would be put at risk by too close an association through the euro with the European economic laggards who had not understood the contemporary direction of economic history.

It is difficult to overstate the extent to which events have disproved this initially plausible analysis. In so far as Britain did in recent years have a distinctive economic model, its characteristics are now shown to have been dangerous errors. It is difficult to believe that the British financial sector will ever again be the provider of jobs, income and tax revenue that it has been in recent years. As a result of the reckless and speculative boom in the least substantial areas of the British economy over the past decade, Mr. Brown's legacy to his successors has been one of debt and economic instability.

In another political culture than that of the United Kingdom, the opposition might well have wished to take advantage of this collapse of Mr. Brown's reasoning which led him to remain outside the euro. Mr. Brown's political opponents could have understood that to force him to reconsider the question of British membership of the European single currency would be a peculiarly potent admission of political and economic defeat from New Labour. But Mr. Cameron's Conservatives were constrained from brandishing this powerful weapon with which to assault the government, not merely by their own visceral Euroscepticism but by the political choices and the rhetoric they employed throughout the whole course of Mr. Brown's chancellorship.

Between 1997 and Mr. Cameron's accession to power in 2005, Euroscepticism was the undisputed motivating force of all the Conservative Party's political action. Mr. Cameron is no enthusiast for the European Union, but does understand that the electorate are easily bored or alarmed by obsessional concentration on the European issue. Under his predecessors, however, the vainglorious claims of Mr. Brown that the British economy was demonstrably outstripping its European neighbours received nothing like the critical scrutiny that they deserved. The idea that continental European economic structures were inferior to those of the United Kingdom, assiduously promoted by Mr. Brown, was one deeply congenial to the Eurosceptic Conservative Party. That this idea reinforced Mr. Brown's unwillingness seriously to contemplate British membership of the euro could only render this fundamentally flawed analysis yet more attractive. German observers politely concealed their scepticism. They knew that strong economies, such as that of Germany, benefit from the stability and predictability within the single European market which the single currency brings. It is striking how rarely British politicians and commentators are willing to acknowledge this reality or the advantages that participation in the euro would bring to a supposedly strong economy such as that of the United Kingdom.

As a result, the Conservative Party supported in opposition precisely those elements of the Prime Minister's general economic approach which are now shown to have been fundamentally flawed. There were not many Conservative spokesmen in recent years arguing that the oft-praised American economic model was one bringing considerable risk to a medium-sized economy such as that of the United Kingdom. Mr. Cameron's and Mr.

Osborne's attempts to draw a clear line between them and Mr. Brown on the question of new debt were a relatively recent development and a clear attempt to distract attention from the fact that their Party has been at least as much in prey as Mr. Brown since 1997 to the myth of a robust, successful British economy striding purposefully ahead of its sluggish continental competitors. The explicit rejection of this myth would have led Mr. Cameron and his Eurosceptic Party along what would be for them dangerous paths.

The 'Westminster consensus' on the subject of the euro has also gained in recent years a new recruit in the form of the Liberal Democrats, traditionally the most pro-European party of the British political spectrum. The document on party policy adopted at their party conference in September 2008 could say no more than that 'there may before long be a case for a renewed hard-headed debate' on the issue. As the representation of the Liberal Democrats has grown in Westminster, their MPs have sought increasingly to adapt themselves to the insular preoccupations and prejudices of the House of Commons. Liberal Democrat MPs have in consequence become more and more reluctant to differentiate themselves from the British Parliamentary mainstream by unseemly displays of enthusiasm for the European Union. This process of blending into the culture of the House of Commons has been reinforced by the fact that a substantial proportion of Liberal Democrats come from the supposedly Eurosceptic South West of England. Many of these MPs believe that their chances of re-election will be improved if they are seen to distance themselves from what until recently was party orthodoxy.

This sea change was well illustrated by their ambiguous attitude to the Lisbon Treaty when it passed through the House of Commons in February, 2008. A substantial proportion of Liberal Democrat MPs were willing and eager to join with the Conservative Party in calling for a referendum on the Treaty, at a time when their leader, Nick Clegg, was vigorously arguing against one. Developments since that time mean that the Liberal Democrat Party is unlikely in any foreseeable future to be an effective standard-bearer for renewed consideration of early membership of the euro. In the last two years, opponents of British membership of the euro believe that their position has been reinforced by the sovereign debt crisis, a view vigorously encouraged by their Eurosceptic friends in the mass media.

These last ten years of silence or evasion on the euro from those whose inner convictions were at variance with their public stances did much more to undermine rational debate on European issues in the United Kingdom than even the previous decade of Mrs Thatcher's growing hostility to all things European and John Major's ineffectual manoeuvrings to hold together an imploding Conservative Party. The events of this period should be a warning and provide lessons of the dangers arising from an excess of self-censorship and reluctance to stake out clear positions on European issues. There are powerful and well-organised forces within the United Kingdom utterly determined to frustrate British membership of the euro. The path towards that membership, if finally undertaken, will in any event be a long and difficult one. There is no reason to believe that it will become easier or less demanding through further postponement. If only proponents of British membership of the euro had shown or would show now the same energy and commitment which the euro's opponents have displayed over the past decade!

In their eagerness to gloat at the economic problems of the Eurozone, the Eurosceptic establishment of this country are all too eager to ignore the entirely comparable economic problems of the United Kingdom. Tragically, the possibility of a British economic catastrophe in the short or medium term can no longer be dismissed out of hand. It is still unclear how severe a bill will be presented for a decade of economic incontinence. The Prime Minister is currently presenting an account of his own failed economic stewardship in which the crisis of the Eurozone looms large as a constraining factor on the British economy. This rationalisation can carry little weight with fair-minded observers, conscious of the counter-productive effects of the Coalition's economic choices. Those favourable to British membership of the euro believe, by contrast, that an impending economic disaster for this country could be mitigated, perhaps even warded off entirely, by Britain's joining the euro, or at least setting out a credible timetable for doing so. This is not a policy that can be implemented overnight. It will require political and economic preparation that needs to be set in hand as soon as possible.

The 60th anniversary of the Schuman Declaration in 2010 brought back to the centre of attention its prescient words that Europe will be built 'through concrete achievements which first create a de facto solidarity'. That powerful sentence was itself a successful blueprint for the first fifty years of the European Union's development. Many of the single currency's most enthusiastic original advocates saw the euro precisely in this light, as an overarching concrete achievement which would substantially reinforce the de facto solidarity of the European Union. Some, such as Chancellor Kohl, saw it as marking a qualitative change in the degree of solidarity upon which the Union was based, a degree of solidarity which he thought was sufficient to make irreversible the integration of the reunited Germany in European institutional structures.

The euro has been in some measure an integrative tool for the Union, but it has suffered from its limited institutional structure, with only the European Central Bank functioning as a genuinely European institution at the level of the Eurozone. When the euro was set up in the late 1990s, national governments, not least the German government, were eager to retain for themselves the greatest possible autonomy of macro-economic decision-making even within the framework of the Eurozone. The Growth and Stability Pact was their attempt to provide a certain minimal supra-national structure of governance for the Eurozone, without setting up any central institution that could be regarded as a direct competitor with national governments in their responsibility for economic policy-making. The inadequacies of the Pact as the basis upon which economic policy-making is conducted at the level of the Eurozone were demonstrated in the early years of the twenty-first century by the regularity with which its provisions were set aside; and more recently by the cumbrous and uncertain response of the Eurozone to the sovereign debt crisis.

When the sovereign debt crisis began in early 2010, those most mindful of the Schuman Declaration's predictions hoped that the crisis would lead to enhanced 'de facto' solidarity. Such hopes have not been disappointed. Faced with the convulsions of the financial markets sparked by the Greek budgetary crisis, the members of the Eurozone have shown themselves capable of acting together to confront the most immediate dangers. No objective observer could believe that its problems have been definitively solved, rather than palliated for the short term. There still remain radical differences of opinion as to the future structure of its governance. Some governments fully understand the intellectual and political tension between the existence of a single European currency on the one hand and the continuation of essentially untrammelled national macro-economic policies on the other.

Against this must be set however the growing realisation over the past two years of heads of state and government that within a single currency zone instrumental integration is the order of the day. Is the Greek dilemma a lone example of unusual fiscal and financial indiscipline or part of a general malaise affecting other deficit countries? Tardily and perhaps reluctantly, the Eurozone's governments have eventually acted in the common interest and there is no reason to believe they will not continue to do so.

There is scope for legitimate debate about how the mechanisms of Eurozone governance might be improved. There is no more urgent task than to convince the national leaders of the Union, in whose hands these decisions rest, that the future of the euro depends on their ability to rise above the calls of narrow nationalism and to pursue their enlightened self-interest by creating new and lasting structures for economic action in common rather than separately. This is the direction in which today's euro and the Schuman Declaration of sixty years ago ineluctably point.

Sadly, Britain can play no part in that debate. Its single contribution thus far has been to lecture our partners on the desirability of establishing a fiscal union between themselves and then to do its (unsuccessful) best to prevent its partners from taking the necessary steps to bring it about. Our partners viewed with incredulity the negotiating tactics of Mr. Cameron at the European Council in December 2011. Far from wishing to be a helpful and constructive participant in discussions which Mr. Cameron himself recognises are of crucial importance for the Eurozone and the United Kingdom alike, Mr. Cameron was more eager to appease the most truculent members of his own Party by making unrealistic and peremptory demands as a 'compensation' for his willingness to act in the common interest with his partners.

The saga of developing British attitudes to European questions in the past twenty years is one full of paradoxes and contradictions. There are few European issues in which these paradoxes and contradictions are more manifest than that of the single European currency. The success or failure of this currency is crucial to the economic future of the United Kingdom; Britain has technical, economic and political expertise to offer which could certainly help the single currency to function more satisfactorily; Britain's remaining outside a more closely integrating Eurozone is a policy which is leading ineluctably towards British isolation within a European Union which we have freely joined in order to work more closely with our partners. None of these pressing considerations however seem to exercise any influence on the self-regarding and short-sighted processes of British Parliamentary politics. To place in jeopardy the United Kingdom's central political and economic interests, when those interests could by a more enlightened and coherent approach be so much better defended is much worse than a crime, it is a flagrant and self-destructive error. That persistence in this error is so enthusiastically endorsed by the British political establishment is truly astonishing. Those whom the gods wish to destroy, they now raise to high positions in British political and parliamentary life.

Chapter Eleven:
Foreign Policy: how to be a world player

The European Union has gone to great pains since the Lisbon Treaty to construct the skeleton of a viable collective foreign policy system. How has this gone down with our Europhobic friends?

As usual most of the press in Britain roundly denounced the creation of the EU External Action Service (EEAS), the posts of President of the European Council and the reinforcement in powers for High Representative for Foreign Affairs and Security Policy. Their shrill objections were not only directed at the impertinent treaty texts themselves. Much outrage was expressed that Europe and the UK government did not choose as the first President of the European Council the totally unsuitable Tony Blair. Insult was added to injury by the choice in his stead of a former Belgian Prime Minister, Mr. Van Rompuy. The latter was well known in other member states but unknown to the British press (not famous for their detailed knowledge of matters European). Objections were moreover raised to the nomination of the British peer Cathy Ashton as High Representative. The Murdoch press and other like-minded tycoons hate it when British politicians ignore their instructions!

Yet there is perhaps a much greater underlying acceptance of the roles of the EEAS amongst MPs and in general than might have been expected, although admittedly it is very early days indeed. The Union's official aims of supporting stability, promoting human rights and democracy, spreading prosperity, good governance and the rule of law, sound irritatingly politically correct. However they can have real resonance amongst struggling Third World populations, who can so easily see a better world available via the web and the internet. The ignorance of yesteryear has faded thanks to world-wide technology. Hopefully, too, the ideals of the Union's Common Foreign and Security Policy will gradually gain acceptance as being helpful policy instruments in a world showing increasing reluctance to rely on the erratic policies of the US, be they in Iraq, Afghanistan or Iran.

The fact that a British nominee, Baroness Ashton, chairs the Foreign Affairs Council of Ministers should reassure the critics, if they are willing to be reassured, that the Union distinguishes between external policies applied by all or most member states – no doubt a growing number of examples – and those cases where a single member state has its own legitimate non-common external policy interest. Examples of the latter will be rare in the practical world of effective collective policy creation. France and

Britain may decide to keep their defence links on an exclusively bilateral base, and Nato has a role to play as well, as we saw in Libya. But such cases will be the exception rather than the rule. In the Ivory Coast France had its own special position, but even this had been certificated by the UN, as the Foreign Minister, Alain Juppé, was quick to emphasise. A similar instance could possibly apply to Britain regarding the Falklands, although here the various initiatives in the UN have had a somewhat different texture, with Argentina gaining some support in principle.

This developing scene has gained greater traction with the positive 'official' stance of the European Parliament, once their early demands for participation in the budget and personnel oversight were met, despite the incessant moaning of the UKIP and the right-wing Tory lobby there. Later even some of the EP Tories in July 2010, now of course members of the new smaller right-wing group, felt obliged to admit ruefully 'we were opposed to the EEAS, but now feel reconciled to engaging constructively within the new architecture, in the best interests of our country'. This astonishing assertion went down like a lead balloon with their Euro-hostile counterparts in the House of Commons. Meanwhile Lady Ashton has adhered to the Community principle of taking on board half the officials from the Council and Commission respectively, and to keep gender balance if possible, subject only to trying to hire the 'brightest'. The Labour government stressed before the last election that the EEAS would complement the national diplomatic services, with the insurance policy of Declaration 14 attached to the new Treaty, which protected all the legal bases of the national foreign services. Noticeably, some smaller member states welcome the new service as a 'sovereignty and power enhancer'.

The British Foreign Secretary, William Hague, in the meantime has had to admit that the world is a different place when you are in government, albeit only a coalition. The Europe Minister, David Lidington, went out of his way to praise the High Representative, in a speech on Bastille Day in 2011! The Tories in government have seemingly continued with their grudging approach of going along with 'something already in the treaty' much to the distaste of quite a few of their own Commons members.

A number of years must pass before the EEAS and the new all-member missions will show their mettle and usefulness in different scenarios and areas. Costs can be kept down realistically by building on the already established history of administrative sharing of staffs and buildings at subordinate levels of activity. A review is agreed for 2014. At the higher levels of decision-making, gaps and question marks remain. The Middle East Quartet was almost as hopeless as the US itself in never managing to get Israel to obey international law vis-à-vis Palestine. The EU part of this quartet must take its share of responsibility for this lack of achievement, apart from the Union's brief monitoring of the Rafah crossing into Gaza, and the German Navy's sea patrols off the Lebanese coast.

The supreme task remains of getting the member states to agree on a combined external policy objective. Here the main culprits are usually the bigger members (except for the disconcertingly agonising and incomprehensible muddle in the long-running Cyprus dispute, which must rank as one of the world's most unnecessary diplomatic stalemates). A cohesive, unanimous EU policy stance would surely have an effect in sorting out seemingly intractable disputes where local and regional interests are clashing.

Working together within the EU framework is always going to impress the external world more than one country going it alone, a reality that right-wing British newspapers refuse to accept. The Georgia mission was a good case in point. Often there will be co-operation between the UN, EU, OSCE, Russia and China to achieve good results when third countries request help. Some of these complex problems will involve responses from the European Union to establish or reinforce human rights outside the Union. If countries ask for guidance in protecting, for example, women's rights, then hopefully even the British Eurosceptics will grudgingly concede that new multinational initiatives need joint action with the EU.

Will they accept, however, the need for Europe-wide human rights structures inside the Union itself? That is yet another psycho-fear of our peculiar band of EU-haters in Britain. For they do not like these trends a bit. Part of this antipathy is to do with our thousand-years-of-history obsession with the claim that human rights started exclusively in Britain. Magna Carta – which incidentally only gave rights of audience to land barons – was at least in the eyes of a certain kind of British patriot the very beginning of parliamentary democracy, unique to us. There is no harm in being proud of these historical events except when the belief persists that no other countries had similar rites of passage. Right-wing anti-EU propagandists repeatedly assert that Britain is a much stronger democracy than any other member state. Norman Tebbit said as much about France to one of the authors many years ago in a Sky TV Target programme debate on the EC, with the vociferously anti-EU

Austin Mitchell MP agreeing eagerly. Many Conservative MPs reject the very notion of the EU being collectively involved in both internal and external human rights.

The EU's commitment to human rights is founded in the Treaty of European Union (TEU) and the Charter of Fundamental Rights. The latter was part of the Treaty of Nice signed in December 2000. Apart from restrictions on the powers of the European Court of Justice in Britain, Poland and the Czech Republic, the Treaty of Lisbon has made the Charter binding.

It is worth recalling that it was John Major who summoned up enough courage – just - to enforce the passage of the Maastricht Treaty that decreed that all citizens were henceforth citizens of the EU as well as their own country. So all individuals everywhere within the member states have the right now to full protection as an EU citizen, the use of the 'citizens initiative', standing and voting in EP and local elections anywhere, full freedom of movement and residence, diplomatic protection outside the EU by any member mission, and appeals to the EU Ombudsman if any EU bodies are apparently guilty of maladministration. All this drives Eurosceptics in Britain apoplectic. How dare these foreigners interfere? But how can it be unacceptable to create friendly new structures of mutual support between member states which give an often remote citizen, anywhere, greater scope for a right of redress? The former Warsaw Pact countries now in the Union, with the occasional exception of Poland, find no difficulty in accepting these arguments.

The Council of Europe, created in 1949, is coming together with the EU, in relevant areas, out of sheer international common sense, without either trespassing on the other's lawn. The 1950 European Convention on Human Rights (ECHR) is a particular target of xenophobic criticism in this country. Some British Tory MPs are constantly clamouring for our own Bill of Rights, which would indeed conflict with the ECHR, itself warmly endorsed by Winston Churchill. This new breed of right-wing, chauvinistic, Conservative MPs, do not always distinguish in their attacks between the ECHR and the European Union. Although not all Council of Europe members are EU members, they are all parties to the ECHR, as they have to be in order to join the former body.

There are further complications to trap the unwary. For instance the EU is not yet, as a collectivity, a party to the ECHR. However all member states of the Union must respect the convention when applying EU law and it is also writ large in the Treaties (Article (3)), as one of the 'general principles' of Union law. The EU is now, as a collectivity, a party to the ECHR. All member states of the Union must respect the Convention when applying EU law etc on joint programmes to advance the rule of law and democracy.

For a country labouring under the absence of a written constitution like the United Kingdom such structures should be seen as a godsend. Many people in Britain do not see it like that, largely as a result of the press barrage. The EU Charter has much wider scope than the ECHR, in terms of social rights, workers rights, data protection, rights to a judge, and similar areas. We are now at the stage when the Union is becoming a contracting party to the ECHR, allowing any EU citizen to apply to the ECHR Court in Strasbourg if they consider that they have had no result from applying to national courts for redress against infringements of EU law by the EU's own institutions.

In the winter of 2010 there was a great deal of protest by the more extreme Tories in the Commons against what they saw as a nexus of continental plots. They sought to leave the ECHR and have our own national bill of rights – this was directly 'encouraged' by David Cameron – and, second, to ignore the EU's own accession to the ECHR with a specific British opt-out. Mr. Lidington, the EU Minister, aided and abetted this ambiguous approach, designed to contain the most militant critics, by switching the UK ratification machinery for accession by the EU away from the EU Amendment Act 2008 to the more abstruse Constitutional Reform and Governance Act 2010.

Once again we were able to witness the striking reality that – apart from a few Polish and Czech moments of uncertainty in these complex processes – the only stuttering antics of resistance were unleashed on a bemused or apathetic public by a British coalition government eager to appease its hardliners. Without exception all the other member countries were enthusiastically in favour. How sad that traditional British statecraft has fallen to such miserably low levels.

Chapter Twelve:
Britain in Europe: neither in nor out

Over the past twenty years, a dangerous experiment has been carried out in the United Kingdom. There has been a futile attempt to combine formal British membership of the European Union with detachment from its main policies, such as the single currency and the Schengen area. This has involved a grudging political acceptance by the British political classes of the rational need for Britain to be part of the Union, offset by ever deeper popular hostility to the Union and everything it stands for. The motives which led to this strange combination of attitudes were various. Lazy and cowardly politicians were able to emphasise, as it served their case, the pro-European or the anti-European side of the argument in their rhetoric and party programmes. A certain tenuous unity within the main political parties could apparently be maintained by this systematic split-personality approach. Some at least of those who acquiesced in it privately believed that when the ambiguities inherent in Britain's tortured relationship with the European Union were finally resolved, it would be to their advantage.

We now know that those from the Eurosceptic side of the argument who embraced the latter analysis have been proved right. Britain is teetering on the brink of resolving its incoherent European policies in favour of at best long-term semi-detachment, perhaps complete separation from the European Union. A heavy price is being paid for the insouciance with which those who have styled themselves as pro-Europeans in Britain over the past decades have always been ready to postpone indefinitely a principled defence and advocacy of a full role for the United Kingdom within the structures of the European Union. We now see the consequences of this emotional and political feebleness, which always stood in flagrant contrast to the emotional and political commitment of the anti-Europeans. The summer of 2011 has shown, a year after the Coalition government was formed, a crystallisation of British public and political opinion hostile to the European Union which must put Britain's continuing membership of the Union in serious doubt. The European Council of December 2011 was in retrospect a foreseeable culmination of this process.

In truth, the first year of the Coalition government showed marked echoes of the wilful self-deceptions which have littered the British debate on Europe in recent British history. The unsavoury appeasement of the Eurosceptics in the Conservative Party under the Major government, which allowed them to hijack the traditionally most pro-

European leading party of British politics; the endless ambiguities of New Labour's policy, the damaging effects of which many pro-Europeans long refused to acknowledge; and the noticeable drift towards Euroscepticism in the Liberal Democrat Party, a drift partly disguised by the rhetoric of some of its leaders - all these tawdry compromises have foreshadowed a qualitative change in the nature of Britain's membership of the European Union. The Coalition's European policy has been all the more insidiously threatening to Britain's position in the European Union because in the first months of the new Coalition, it was carried out discreetly. Initially, the Coalition did not seek confrontation for the sake of confrontation, but nevertheless worked remorselessly to shift the intellectual and political basis on which European debate is conducted in the United Kingdom.

Twenty years of anti-European propaganda in the British mass media, silence by British pro-European forces and the crisis of the Eurozone have interacted with the attitudes of the most Eurosceptic British government in a generation to create something very like a new anti-European consensus in this country. This consensus is reflected in the current British European debate, which takes for granted that Britain will not be in any foreseeable future a full member of the European Union. The current British debate revolves rather around the extent of British withdrawal from the European Union, whether it should be complete or merely partial. The role in government of the supposedly pro-European Liberal Democrat Party has been to provide some apparent political cover for this process. In private, its leading spokesmen have even claimed some credit for slowing down developments which would otherwise have been yet more destructive. Those who wish to be deceived will always find ways of deceiving themselves.

The sombre history of the passage of the European Union Bill through Parliament last summer was a perfect example of this phenomenon. Liberal Democrat MPs were won over by Mr. Cameron's propagandistic arm-twisting to support the Bill on all votes. All the amendments proposed by the Lords to mitigate some of the more absurd effects of a wholly destructive and appalling Bill were rejected by the Commons. As The Guardian put it on 7th December 2010, it was 'a shameful moment to see … the most pro-European party, and ….Tories such as Kenneth Clarke trooping in to the lobbies….in support of such a foolish and feckless and futile Bill.'

The disappearance of the Liberal Democrats as an even theoretically pro-European force should not be underestimated as a blow. Sadly, there is no politically organised current of British opinion today that aspires to join the single European currency at any stage in the future. There is no politically organised force that wishes to reverse the practical disadvantages of Britain's self-exclusion from the Schengen area; or that regards the range of British 'opt-outs' from the European treaties as damaging rather than helpful for our country's true national interests.

On the contrary, a Eurosceptic mythology is becoming every day more powerful in the British political debate, a mythology founded on implausible but enthusiastically advocated claims about the imminent demise of the single

European currency and the systematic reversal of the extraordinary achievements of European integration since the Treaty of Rome. The construction of this mythology is clearly being prepared to justify and to reinforce yet further psychological and political estrangement of the United Kingdom from the European Union. The very notion of pooling sovereignty, a concept at the very heart of the Union is routinely denounced and denigrated by even prestigious commentators and mainstream politicians in the United Kingdom.

The comment and reporting surrounding the European Council of June 2011 may stand as one example for many of this terrible evolution. In the week of the Council, a string of articles appeared in the widest range of newspapers casting the deepest doubts on the future of the euro. Few if any attempts were made by journalists to recall the long-standing and considerable efforts devoted by the members of the Eurozone to confronting the consequences of the global financial crisis for the single European currency. Nor was any differentiation made between different possible outcomes and their implications for the Eurozone as a whole.

The assumption of all these articles was that the single European currency was doomed and that the refusal of European leaders to recognise this manifest certainty was simply another manifestation of their feckless stupidity. The British press is bizarrely proud of the now well-established tradition of regular devaluations to get the United Kingdom out of balance-of-payment and debt difficulties. It gives no heed to the obvious truth that a regime of competing national currencies in Europe after the financial crisis of 2008 would have led to economic crisis in our continent on a vast scale.

Self-deceptive and caricatural attitudes were also much in evidence in the media reporting about the Schengen arrangement, now a well-established pillar of European integration. Difficulties affecting a small minority of travellers in a small minority of countries were regularly presented by British commentators in the summer of 2011 as foretelling the universal reintroduction of national frontiers. One of the most prominent correspondents of the Financial Times, Philip Stephens, intoned in his column a funeral oration over the whole concept of European sovereignty-sharing. Interestingly, his more recent columns have shown an awareness of the at least premature nature of this obituary; and a recognition of the disastrous consequences of the disintegrative developments he seemed to be predicting.

Such a hysterical campaign of denigration bears little or no relation to the objective circumstances of the European Union. The difficulties posed by the interaction of the inadequate governance structures of the euro and the consequences of the global financial crisis have created real problems for the Union and the Eurozone. In times of economic difficulty, there are always siren voices claiming that short-sighted selfishness and national solutions are more likely to be successful than co-operative action. But any reasonable observer would have to recognise that, in these times of economic travails and popular uncertainty, it is striking how well the Union has held together rather than how much it has regressed from its ideals.

This is every bit as applicable to the Schengen arrangement as it is to the single European currency. Without the euro, the consequences for the economic life of Europe, including the United Kingdom, would have been catastrophic. The expectation that Europe's leaders will put at risk such an achievement is wholly far-fetched. In the same way, millions of Europeans daily benefit from the ease of travel and communication assured by the Schengen system. Marginal and transitional problems are extremely unlikely to reverse so obviously successful and rationally progressive a development. The loving care with which the problems of the Eurozone and the problems of the Schengen system are described at such length in the British media says much more about the view the British would like to take of the European Union than about the Union itself.

There is a long and discreditable tradition in the United Kingdom of underestimating the seriousness of the commitment of our continental neighbours to the process of European integration. There are remarkable echoes in today's European debate of the scepticism with which the British ruling classes greeted the aspirations of the Messina Conference and the Treaty of Rome. It is as if the intervening years, with all the progress made towards European unification despite British obstructionism, had never taken place. There is a persistent British resentment that the losing European powers of the Second World War in north western Europe found it so much easier than did the United Kingdom to put behind them the trauma of that period and evolve for themselves a fundamentally new set of relationships in Europe.

A favoured complaint of Eurosceptics is that European integration is proceeding undemocratically, with insufficient consultation of national voters. What is usually meant is that democratically elected governments in Europe do not always allow themselves to be browbeaten by sectional or demagogic currents of opinion to pursue the irrationality of short-term nationalistic policies. Those advocating such policies are eager to disguise their dubious motives in the cloak of democracy, or at least one version of democracy. It is no coincidence that the version of democracy most favoured by Eurosceptics throughout the European Union is that of the referendum. Notoriously, referendums are vulnerable to precisely the eddies and incoherence of public opinion which representative democracy is designed to avoid. The European Union is very definitely a product of representative democracy. Its creation does great credit to this form of democracy. It is indeed a conclusive demonstration of the superiority of representative government to the dangerous irrationality of demagoguery.

Ironically, the fears of the Eurosceptic media may turn out to be correct, although certainly not in the way they think. There is a real danger that, without proper public discussion or consultation, Britain's position within the European Union is being increasingly eroded by the conscious decision of the majority party in the governing Coalition, a decision accepted without protest, or even awareness, by the minority party in the Coalition. This book is a protest against the individual misconceptions about the European Union and its policies which have led to this dangerous position. It is also a warning that Britain is nearer to leaving the European Union than many observers believe.

If this disastrous outcome is to be avoided, it is urgently necessary for those who know that Britain has no acceptable future outside the Union to realise the gravity of the position in which we find ourselves. We must take lessons from our opponents about the need for organised, effective and determined campaigning action. Our opponents have never been willing to allow their anti-European case to be lost by default. Pro-Europeans have come perilously close in the past twenty years to allowing just that to happen to their cause. Complacency is a luxury that pro-Europeans in this country can emphatically no longer afford.

Nor need pro-Europeans give way to despair. The virus of Euroscepticism is one which primarily affects politicians and the press. The general public are far more intelligent and sophisticated than either of these self-regarding groups. The growing mobility, especially of younger UK citizens, around the other member states for a range of reasons ranging from mere backpacking to study, jobs and marriage, is slowly and unobtrusively creating a new generation of 'natural' rather than 'self-conscious' Europeans. These young people do not yet make the decisions which govern British responses to present and new EU initiatives. But opinion polls show greater support for the Union among the young than among their elders.

It would be a shabby inheritance of the older generation to deprive the new generation of their ability to participate fully in the political and economic future of Europe, their continent. An isolated, self-pitying, self-righteous and enfeebled (dis)United Kingdom is at the time of writing an entirely plausible legacy for our children. They do not want, need or deserve this legacy. Time is running out to offer them a better future.

Appendix
Euro myths and the real world

Interested readers will recall our chapter on the huge number of UK press and website examples, highlighting the latest dastardly attacks on our heroic freedoms.

We set out below some examples of these stories.

12/01/2009 Mail and Express
EU to ban plasma TV sets

24/05/2009 Mail
EU to ban watts on light bulbs

26/06/2009
EU to ban Dunkirk hero boats from UK ports

09/08/2009 News of the World

UK paid £16.3 billion in 2008

28/10/2009 Express
EU secret plans to levy direct income tax

16/12/ 2009 Express
EU to prohibit bingo callers from using colloquial phrases

11/01 2010 Telegraph
EU commission is operating illegally

19/03/2010 Telegraph
EU Commission wasting £366m in 2010 on "culture"

06/04/2010 Mail
EU Commission wants to abolish English Channel name

07/06/2010 Sun
Brussels tries to stop Britain going metric

27/06/2010 Mail Telegraph and others
EP to ban selling eggs in Britain by the dozen

08/07/2010 Mail
Brussels fines UK £150m for failing to fly EU flag

08/07/2010 Express
EU plans to liquefy human remains for drain disposal

27/07/2010 Telegraph
EU culture bureaucrats waste £400m on secret payments
20/08/2010 Telegraph

EU Commission dictates contents of Cornish pasties

29/09/2010 Mail
EU officials force Cadbury's to drop "glass and a half"

24/10/2010 News of the World
EU splurges £158m on vocational training in 2011

28/10/2010 Telegraph
EU officials hijack Britain's Remembrance Sunday

All of these "stories" were just that.